Simple ways to create powerful,

personal messages that

✔ thank the people who've
   helped you in the past

✔ apologize to those you
   may have hurt

✔ offer practical advice for
   now and for later

✔ inspire, comfort and
   leave others feeling
   cherished

✔ invite people to think
   of you with love and a
   smile

✔ help you get over your
   reluctance to do this

from Me to You

The reluctant writer's guide to powerful, personal messages

JacLynn Morris &

Paul L. Fair, Ph. D.

WRITER'S DIGEST BOOKS

Cincinnati, Ohio
www.writersdigest.com

Visit our Web site at www.writersdigest.com for information on more resources for writers.

To receive a free weekly E-mail newsletter delivering tips and updates about writing and about Writer's Digest products, send an E-mail with "Subscribe Newsletter" in the body of the message to: newsletter-request@writersdigest.com, or register directly at our Web site at www.writersdigest.com.

04 03 02 01 00   5 4 3 2 1

Library of Congress Cataloging in Publication Data

Morris, JacLynn
    From me to you: the reluctant writer's guide to powerful, personal messages / by JacLynn Morris and Paul L. Fair
        p.   cm.
Includes index.
    ISBN 1-58297-004-1 (alk. paper)
    1. Letter writing 2. Interpersonal communication. I. Fair, Paul L. II. Title.
PE1483.M58 2000   00-043653
808.6--dc21   CIP

Edited by Meg Leder
Cover and interior design by Matthew S. Gaynor
Cover photography by ©2000 Tony Stone
Production coordinated by Emily Gross

Greeting card text on page 35 reprinted by permission of Recycled Paper Greetings, Inc. © Original design by Bugs Herbert. All rights reserved.

Acknowledgments

A Special Message of Thanks to Those Who Helped Us Along the Way

As we sat leafing through our completed manuscript, we thought about all of you—the men and women we met, interviewed, laughed and cried with along the way. So many of you nurtured us and helped us shape the pages in this book. You entrusted us with your joys, sorrows, successes and embarrassments, and we are enormously grateful. You have made this book a joy to write.

Thank you,

JacLynn and Paul

They laughed, they cried, they became a part of this:
Elizabeth Arnold; Peggy Baker; Rosemary Barnes; Aaron, Amy, Beverly, Bruce, David, Ed, Ellen, Gary, Iris, Jodi, Kent, Linda and Mildred Beckwith; Candy and Steve Berman; Iris Bolton, Ph.D.; Stefan Cohen; Perle R. Corn; Cathleen Cueto; Carrell A. Dammann, Ph.D.; Tom Duncanson; Marcia Dworetz; Denise and Eddie Esserman; Mary Ann Fair; JoAnne and Stuart Finestone; Viki Freeman; Roni Funk, MSW; Gail Gordon; Linda Gordon; Sherry Haber; Harold W. Haddle Jr., Ph.D.; Jack Halpern; Kate Hamilton, MSW, CISW; Rachel Hammer; A. Neil Harrison, M.D.;Debbie Harrison; Leah, Mark, Sharon and Robert Harrison; Harlyn and Maurice Joseph; Al Kitchen; Rabbi Phil Kranz; Jill Krischer; Stanley M. Lefco; Harriet and Henry Leibowitz; Charla and Steve Lerman; Debbie Levinson; Wendy Lipshutz; Amy Lively; Benjamin C. Mathes Jr.; Barbara Skutch Mays; Patty Maziar; Anita Maziar Morris; Vimala Nair, M.D.; Jim Nathan; Liza Nelson; Vicki Otten; Christopher Patterson; Nancy Polonsky; Brook Raflo; Agnes Rizzo; Frank Rizzo; Ellen Yanuck Rosenbloom; Denise Sanders; Margaret (Peggy) Saxon; Rabbi Ronald M. Segal; S. Stephen Selig III; Susan Shaffer; Esther Solin;Robyn Freedman Spizman; Colette and Yvonne Stern; Harry D. Stern;Fran Tarkenton; Nick Taylor; Marshall Thurber; Hope Tudanger; Kathryn Yanuch Wenger; Martha Yoder; Bobbi Zarin; Susan Zohlman.

They inspired us:
Murray Bowen, M.D.; A remarkable place called Canyon Ranch in Tucson, Arizona; Scott Gibbs and all who work at Atlanta's Caribou Coffee at Powers Ferry Square.

They held our hands, hugged our hearts and cheered us on:
Virginia and Alexandra Cueto; Michael Mandel; Bruce, Peter and Emily Morris; Caryl M. Paller.

They advised with wisdom, edited with care and published with enthusiasm:
Meredith Bernstein; Jack Heffron; Meg Leder; Richard Rosenthal.

JacLynn Morris is a freelance writer, public speaker and business consultant. She holds a master's degree in educational counseling from Boston University. Currently she lives in Atlanta, where she is writing a book, speaking to various groups about the issue of child abuse and conducting message-making workshops. She is happily married to her husband of twenty-two years, Bruce H. Morris, a criminal defense attorney. They have two nearly grown children.

Paul L. Fair, Ph.D., a graduate of Boston University, is a licensed clinical psychologist in private practice. He specializes in stress disorders and individual's and couple's psychotherapy. Currently he lives in Atlanta with his wife, Virginia, a conference logistics professional. They have a grown daughter who is pursuing a career in art education and pottery.

If you would like to share your reactions to this book, please e-mail JacLynn at JacLynnMorris@mail.com or Paul at PaulFair@mail.com.

TABLE OF CONTENTS:

INTRODUCTION

Searching for Answers

$\mathcal{T}$his book came to life over a cup of coffee in the middle of a conversation between two friends—a psychologist and a writer.

Both of us are old enough to remember where we were the day President Kennedy was shot. Neither of us was alive during the Great Depression.

One of us is a small, dark-haired woman who talks with her hands, listens with a smile and speaks to a stranger at the drop of a hat. The other is a tall, light-haired man who leans into his words with quiet, serious intensity. One of us celebrates Christmas. The other lights Chanukah candles.

Together we followed this path of questions:

- What if you thought you might not be here tomorrow?
- What would you say today?
- Why would you want someone to know that?
- Whom would you tell?
- Could you create something that would help other people now and even after you are gone?
- What would it be?

Searching for answers, we set out from different places, for different reasons and with different expectations.

ల౧

JacLynn

I'd asked myself these questions for years. I'd even searched through bookstores hoping to find "something" that showed people how to write down everything they wanted their loved ones to know before they died. And I wanted that "something" to do one more thing—I wanted it to help fill the empty spaces in me.

My father died when I was two and a half years old. I didn't have time to know him. I'm not even sure if he left something of himself behind for me. There was just this big emptiness where my dad should have been and no way to fill it. I struggled to live without whatever it was I was missing.

But when my own children were born, I felt a sudden heart-pounding fear for them. What if I wasn't here tomorrow? What would happen to my children? How much of me would they know? What part of me might they need? How could I make sure they would get it?

As my children grew, I was still concerned for them, but the focus of my questions expanded to include other people I love—my husband, my relatives and my friends. What could I leave behind to let them know how deeply they had affected my life? How could I thank them, comfort them and urge them to go forward? I wrote this book hoping to find out.

⁊

Paul

I grew up in a home where feelings were tightly controlled and seldom discussed. Maybe that's why when my father died a few years ago, my sisters and I left his funeral still wanting to know that we had mattered to him. In his will Dad wrote "Dear Children, I left each of you a personal letter." But he didn't leave us those letters! And his unwritten messages added even more confusion to our profound sense of loss.

I want to do things differently. I want to make sure that my daughter, wife and family know how deeply I love them. I don't want to leave important questions unanswered. I want to find concrete ways to express my feelings, share my memories, pass along some things I've learned and thank the people who have helped me grow.

As a psychologist whose patients grapple with unresolved questions, fears of mortality and misunderstandings—and as a private person who struggles with many of these issues in my own life—I want to start sharing the best of myself in tangible ways right now, before it's too late. But how? I wrote this book hoping to find out.

⁊

Finding easy ways to put our thoughts and feelings on paper was very important to us. So was our desire to show others how to make powerful, personal messages. We want to give you simple steps to follow so that your loved ones will not be left as we were—struggling to live with missing pieces and unanswered questions. That is what led us to write this book.

We started out by telling our friends, families and professional associates what we were trying to do. We watched their eyes grow wide; we heard them catch their breath and saw them nod their heads. They understood. Many of them said they were reluctant to express themselves in writing, but all of them wanted to make messages for the special people in their lives. They encouraged us to move forward with this project. So we began offering a series of workshops, seminars and classes.

With wonderful generosity, our friends, families, the people who came to our message-making workshops and even strangers we met at our favorite coffee shop made suggestions, told us their stories and gave us copies of special messages they had received from others. They also shared with us some of the things they wanted to give to their loved ones now and in the future. We've included many of these along with our own stories and messages in the pages that follow.

At times (and with permission), we have identified the person who created a specific message. In general, however, the people who made the lasting, personal messages that you will find in this book preferred to share their thoughts and feelings anonymously and we have honored their request.

Because they are tangible, these messages can be read, listened to, watched or looked at—over and over again. When people can hold your words in their hands, it is easier for them to recall and reexperience their relationship with you whenever they'd like to—whether you are there with them in person or not.

But perhaps the best thing about putting your thoughts, hopes and feelings for others in concrete form is this: Something about the experience of creating a personal message seems to connect you more deeply with the people in your life right now.

Whether they're based on small, tender moments or on bigger, more dramatic experiences, all the messages in this book are gifts of the heart. We hope they will inspire you to create your own messages and wrap them with care so they can be passed along as lasting gifts for the people you love.

A Father's Gift in Progress

*Jac*Lynn's husband, Bruce, who'd had little experience expressing his feelings on paper, wanted to give his son a graduation card. We thought (and Bruce agreed) that by showing you what happened when he added the basic elements of a special message, which are described more fully for you in the next chapter, you'd see that anyone can do this. It's not hard! As you read Bruce's story, watch how easily a message can grow from ordinary to extraordinary when key elements are added. This is how Bruce described what happened:

> *Two weeks ago, I sat with my wife at our son's high school graduation. For lots of reasons, it was an emotional time for us. My mind reeled back to all that had led up to this moment. I remembered the day Peter was born, the afternoon he was diagnosed with learning disabilities, the time a team of psychologists told us we should lower our expectations of what our son could achieve in life. And all those years when we struggled to help him spell and add and memorize! Now, here I was holding the graduation program where Peter's name was entered next to the words "Cum Laude" graduate.*
>
> *I leaned toward my wife and whispered, "I'm going to buy a special graduation card for Peter and write something in it that he can keep."*
>
> *JacLynn nodded at me and smiled.*
>
> *A day later I bought a card for our son. Inside it I wrote this:*

May 1998
Dear Peter,
You've worked so hard to get to this moment.
Congratulations, I am very proud of you!

When I showed my wife what I'd written, she tried to smile. "OK, what's wrong?" I asked. She told me that what I'd written was "very nice" but that it seemed as though any man might have written it to his son. "Sort of generic" was how she described my message. She said she thought I ought to explain what made me want to write this card in the first place. And that I ought to say more about how I feel about my son, mention some of the things that I really love about him and tell him how I had felt at his graduation. I decided that maybe she was right. Here is what I added:

> At your commencement, I found your name listed among those who'd achieved academic excellence. I was impressed not only by your accomplishments but also by your ability to keep this a surprise. You have always made me proud, and on this occasion, you did so again.

I showed my wife the words I'd added. I thought she'd be as pleased as I was. She wasn't. In fact, she said my message made me sound like a lawyer. "Well I am a lawyer," I snapped back. She sighed and said, "Yes, but not to Peter. To him you're a dad. Wouldn't it be better to write to him the way that you talk to him? I mean, do you really think you'd describe his awesome grades as 'academic excellence'? I don't think so!"

I shrugged and walked away but I knew she was right. So I gave it another try. Here's how I rewrote my message:

> When I sat in the audience at your high school graduation ceremony last week, I grinned the whole time. I can't believe that you kept us in the dark about being a "Cum Laude" graduate.
>
> What a wonderful moment it was for me to open the printed program and read your name right there in the special honors section. I loved the surprise! You have given me a special memory that I will always cherish.
>
> Peter, I love you no matter what, but I also admire you because you are so willing to tackle life's challenges, even the ones that seem overwhelming, like succeeding despite your learning disabilities. No one appreciates how

hard you've worked more than your mom and I do. I am
so glad that I am your father.

*I was just about to sign this card when my wife peeked over my shoulder
and said, "Surely you want to write about some of the things that Peter
went through to get to this special day."*

*She was starting to bug me. But I gave it a shot and added these
words:*

Remember that day when you threw your books across the
kitchen and shouted, "I can't do this! It's too hard! I quit!" I
didn't know what to say to you. I wasn't even sure we
should let you stay in a school where you felt so much pressure. But then, very quietly you picked up all your books
and sat back down to try again. You showed such courage
that day, and you bring that quality to everything you do.

I still recall when you were about three, you had a bad
case of the stomach flu and lay on the bathroom floor in
your superman pajamas. You looked up at me and said,
"Daddy, my superpowers are failing!" Well guess what
son, your superpowers have never been stronger. You are
the cum laude kid supreme!

*Feeling pretty good about myself, I showed what I'd written to JacLynn
again. She smiled and said "That's lovely."*

I looked up at her and said, "Buuuuuut ...?"

*And that's when she admitted that since she and Paul were working on
this book, she wished I would add something to tell Peter what I hoped he'd
get from my words. I grabbed my card back from her, glared and went off.*

*A few days later, I showed her my fifth (and final I mean it, JacLynn!)
draft where I added this:*

Peter, my father used to write notes to me—especially on
Father's Day. His notes said things like, "I know you're
supposed to honor me today, but I feel so fortunate to
have you as a son that I wanted to thank you and tell you
how much I love you." I've kept all his notes, and now
that he's gone, they mean an awful lot to me. But when I
started to write this for you, I wanted to take what my father had given me and add something more to it for you.

I've never done this before. So, I am sitting here at
my desk feeling pretty awkward. But I'm telling you this
so that someday, when it comes time for you to write to

your own children, you will try to add even more to what you pass along to them. Then, this could turn into a family tradition. I'd like that and I bet Poppy would, too. I love you and I am proud that you are my son.

> Love,
> Dad

When I finally gave this graduation card to my son, I felt obligated to tell him that his mother had helped me write some of it. Peter smiled, patted my hand and said, "That's OK, Dad, Mom helps me, too!"

Using Your True Voice

Watching the way Bruce developed a message for Peter showed us how important it is to write from the heart using the kinds of words and phrases that we use in our everyday conversations with people. That is what some people call using your "true voice." Using your true voice means writing without trying to be perfect, without using big words when little ones would work just as well and without glossing over our feelings and thoughts

Certainly, there are times when we'd rather use appropriate or important sounding words. But we have found that whenever we write in our own "true voices," our words resonate in others with greater clarity and impact.

Writing in your true voice also makes it more likely that your messages will

- go beyond polite words, appropriate feelings or greeting card sentiments
- be honest and genuine
- express goodwill
- reveal deep feelings
- communicate the importance and value of your relationship to the receiver.

To show you how writing in your true voice adds power and depth to a message, notice the feeling you have as you read this:

> At your commencement, I found your name listed among those who'd achieved academic excellence. I was impressed not only by your accomplishments but also by your ability to keep this a surprise. You have always made me proud, and on this occasion, you did so again.

Now, compare how that last paragraph made you feel to the way you feel when you read the following:

> When I sat in the audience at your high school graduation ceremony last week, I grinned the whole time. I can't believe that you kept us in the dark about being a "Cum Laude" graduate.
>
> What a wonderful moment it was for me to open the printed program and read your name right there in the special honors section. I loved the surprise! You have given me a special memory that I will always cherish.
>
> No one appreciates how hard you've worked more than your mom and I do. I am so glad that I am your father.

The difference between writing something that sounds appropriate, like the first example, and writing something that touches a person's heart, like the second example often boils down to whether or not you have written in your "true voice," an honest voice that expresses how you really feel.

So, as we move ahead in this book, we will keep reminding you about the value of writing in your true voice and we will point out several messages in which the senders have done a particularly good job of writing in their own true voices.

But what is it that makes some messages feel special? To find out, we looked at hundreds of letters, cards, notes and the like that people we know have cherished and held onto for years. In the beginning, we had assumed that to make messages important enough to have lasting meaning and value for others we would have to write lengthy, strongly worded personal letters. Happily we were wrong.

The Size of a Special Message

Looking closely at all kinds of messages, we were amazed to see that while many of the most deeply connecting ones were long, just as many were short. So, the good news for those of you who are reluctant writers is this: Special messages come in all sizes. *You* get to decide how much you want to write. And depending upon what you are trying to communicate and how deeply you want to delve into a particular topic, your messages can range from three or four sentences to volumes of pages.

Great Messages Come in a Variety of Different Forms

While letter writing offers many advantages, the truth is that powerful, personal messages come in many different forms. So, if you shy away from letter writing, there are plenty of other ways to make lasting messages. For example, some people tape-record themselves telling stories that touched them. Others attach a few words to personal treasures like recipes that have been in their families for years, photos that capture favorite moments, or poems their young children have written. A few people wrap their messages creatively in video-taped greetings, paint words on lampshades or scrawl notes inside hand-drawn greeting cards.

Often, just the fact that a person puts time, effort, thought or originality into something to delight or help us makes a message wonderful.

If you like to write, you can list your ideas in a straightforward manner. Or you might prefer to fill your messages with everything from made-up song lyrics to full descriptions of the lessons you have learned along the way. Some people enjoy bringing messages to life with dialogue. Others let their thoughts flow without a set direction.

Any and all of these different forms and styles can be used to create re-markable and touching messages. There are, however, times when letter writing offers several advantages. It can help you

- share information that seems too difficult to discuss in person
- carefully choose words that convey your intentions most effectively
- focus on your positive feelings
- cope with uncomfortable feelings as they come up
- take the receiver's likely reaction into account
- adjust the flow of information
- check the tone of a message

And it can help the receiver

- take in the message slowly
- react in private and without self-conscious concern for the sender's feelings
- have time to decide how to use the information

What You Will Find in the Next Two Chapters

Having seen how Bruce put a graduation message together for his son, know-ing that powerful messages come in all sizes and forms, and understanding the importance of writing in your own true voice, you may be tempted to jump to some of the chapters in this book that deal with the kinds of messages you are most interested in making. But we strongly recommend that you read the next two chapters before you get underway. Chapter two describes the five basic elements (the same ones that Bruce used) that give structure to all forms, styles, and kinds of personal messages. And chapter three explains two simple techniques that can make this even easier. These chapters will provide you with the basic tools to create your own meaningful messages.

What to Put in Your Messages

$\mathcal{T}$here are five basic elements that make a message powerful, intimate, satisfying and meaningful. Whether you want to thank people, express tender feelings, give advice, apologize, forgive, answer important questions, share a favorite memory or make your wishes known, the key to doing this with clarity and impact is to include all five elements in your message.

What Are the Five Basic Elements?

Simply put, the elements that will make your messages resonate with people are your answers to these questions:

1. What got me thinking about you?
2. What are my positive feelings for you?
3. What makes you special to me?
4. What do I remember and treasure about our time together?
5. What do I want you to get from my message?

To show you how the answers to these questions add depth and value to a message, we are going to look at three versions of a letter written by a woman who came to one of our workshops.

The woman, whom we'll call "Nancy," was kind enough to let us show you what happened when she added each of the basic elements, one by one, into a note she was writing for her fifteen-year-old daughter, "Carrie." At the time, Carrie was away at summer camp.

Nancy created her first draft at the start of our workshop, before we had explained anything about the basic elements. After we described the elements, Nancy created two more versions of her letter. Her second draft will show you a good example of how to apply the five elements. But you will see that when Nancy reworked her letter and made a third version, she did an even better job of incorporating the elements. As we watch her develop this message, we'll look at some of the specific reasons that Nancy's second draft is good and her third one is even better.

Generally speaking, however, the difference between "good" and "even better" has to do with

- the vividness of detail you use when you answer each question
- the degree to which you reveal your feelings
- your use of your own true voice

Element 1: What Got Me Thinking About You?

This element sets the stage for all that is to come. When you apply the *What got me thinking about you?* element at the start of a message, you create an intimate, self-revealing tone that helps the receiver focus more fully on your words. Using this element effectively, calls for you to

- begin with a brief statement about your inner thoughts—something like "I thought about how long it's been since we've seen each other..."
- mention the positive feeling(s) you have when you think of the person, which may be as simple as "I felt lonely for you"
- add details that describe your physical surroundings, "when I looked up at my bookshelf in the den a moment ago and spotted that goofy photo of you and me at last year's reunion"

To give you a better feel for what happens (or more accurately doesn't happen) in people when they read messages that do not include this element, take a look at Nancy's first draft. Keep in mind that she wrote this before she knew about the basic elements of a message:

> July 1999
> Dear Carrie, I haven't heard from you in a long time. Are
> you OK?

There really isn't anything wrong with what Nancy wrote here. In fact, many of us have probably started some of our own letters this way. But what if you were Carrie? What do you imagine her reaction to the first two sentences in this note might be?

Carrie and her mother met with us at the end of the summer. When we showed Carrie the three drafts her mom had written, Carrie told us how she would have felt if she had received the first version of her mother's letter:

> *I'd have been mad. I mean, before I left, Mom said that I should go off and have the best summer of my life and that's what I was doing. If she wanted me to write to her more often, all she had to do was say so in person or write something to tell me how she was missing me. But all that I got out of reading what you just showed me is weirded out and mad because she sounds like she thinks that I've done something wrong. So, I'm glad Mom didn't mail that one to me!*

"So am I!" Nancy told her daughter.

Now take at look at what happened when Nancy rewrote her note using the *What got me thinking about you?* element right off the bat:

> July 1999
> Dear Carrie, I am standing outside your room thinking
> about how much I miss you right now.

In this version, the tenderness that Nancy feels toward her absent daughter is much more apparent. The feelings she expresses ring true. In part, this is because Nancy did a good job of writing in her true voice. But the words "standing outside your room," which describe her physical setting, and the words "I miss you right now," which share her inner experience, are what really lend a gentle, more personal tone to her letter.

Reading this version of her mom's letter, Carrie said, "I like this one a lot better. It's like I can almost hear Mom saying those words, and if she had mailed it to me, I'd have smiled and thought, *Gee, that is so sweet. My mother misses me!*"

Now look at Nancy's third version. Notice that by expanding the description of her surroundings and giving more details about her inner experience, Nancy added impact to her words. This is what she wrote:

> July 1999
> Dear Carrie, I am standing outside your room thinking
> about how much I miss you right now. The house seems
> so quiet—I never thought I'd be telling you this, but I
> even miss the sound of that loud music you play in your
> room when you get home from school. Bet you never ex-
> pected me to say that!

In this version, the picture that Nancy paints for her daughter seems clearer and more complete than it was in her two earlier drafts. Her words "The house seems so quiet" and "I even miss the sound of" make this an even better example of an effective way to use element 1. We also liked the way Nancy described what was going on in the moment without resorting to fluffy adjectives.

When she read this version of her mother's letter, Carrie's response was, "Way cool, Mom!"

Here is what happens when you address the *What got me thinking about you?* element effectively. It

- lets people know that your feelings for them have moved you to write
- creates a vivid image in their minds, which helps them give their full attention to your words
- invites them to notice their own thoughts and feelings about your relationship

Tips for Using Element 1: What Got Me Thinking About You?

Do I need to tell someone what got me thinking about him if the answer is as obvious as it's his birthday?

Even when you're writing to wish someone a happy birthday, it is a good idea to let that person know what you were feeling and thinking about and where you were when you made your message. Why? Because doing that personalizes your message, helps the person feel special and pulls him directly into your experience.

How do I use the *What got me thinking about you?* element in a message when I'm angry at the other person?

When feelings are running high, explaining what prompted you to create a message for the other person helps you describe your feelings in a non-blaming way. And that is what can help the receiver to let go of her defensiveness and feel more willing to let your words in.

Here is a good way to use the *What got me thinking about you?* element in a message about a conflict:

> I hate when we are fighting like this because you are my dearest friend.

Now here is an even better way to use this element in the same situation:

> I hate when we are fighting like this because you are my dearest friend. I am sitting here trying to write this and

my hands are sweating so much that the pen I'm using
keeps slipping out of my hand.

In this instance, the difference between the good and even better examples shows up in the details. In the even better version, the sender added extra details about sweaty hands and the slipping pen; these words form a vivid description and reveal the sender's inner experience in a compelling and clear manner.

How do I write about my feelings without sounding like I'm gushing all over the other person?

When you want your message to fall somewhere between saying too little and going way overboard, here is what can help: Think about what is prompting you to write in the first place. Are you feeling delighted, surprised, sad, gentle or maybe lonely? Name the feeling that comes up inside of you and write it down.

Next, pay attention to your physical reaction to that feeling. Does it leave you teary-eyed? Does it make your stomach drop? Does it make you grin, groan or burst out laughing? Maybe you're feeling so nostalgic that you've started listening to oldies on the radio. Write one or two sentences that describe your physical reaction to your feeling.

Now, look around at your immediate environment. Are you sitting in your favorite chair? Are there pictures nearby of the person you're writing to? Did something on television remind you of this person? Again, jot your answer down in one or two sentences.

That's all you need to do in order to use this element crisply, clearly, truthfully and without going overboard.

Element 2: What Are My Positive Feelings for You?

Answering the question, *What are my positive feelings for you?* means coming right out and telling someone that he is important to you. Even if you think the other person already knows (or should know) how you feel, put it in your message. Everyone appreciates hearing that he is valued.

To understand how meaningful this element is to the receiver, let's look at more of what Nancy wrote in her first draft to Carrie. The words Nancy used here are fine, but they lack emotional weight because element 2 is missing:

Dad and I are fine. How's the food at camp?

When Nancy learned about the basic elements of a special message, she made changes in her note to Carrie. Here is how she applied the *What are my positive feelings for you?* element in her second version:

> I love you very much.

Again, this is a good use of element 2. Nancy's words clearly express how she feels about Carrie. But notice what happens in Nancy's next version where she added more details to describe her feelings:

> Since you've been at camp, I have really missed you. The good part of this is that it lets me know how much I love you.

This version is an even better way to apply the *What are my positive feelings for you?* element. The words "it lets me know how much I love you" communicate much more about the depth of Nancy's feeling. When you put the *What are my positive feelings for you?* element in your messages you

- ✦ leave others no room to doubt your positive feelings for them
- ✦ open them up to notice their own feelings about your relationship

Tip for Using Element 2: What Are My Positive Feelings for You?

What if I like someone but am not going to say, "I love you"? What do I put in my message then?

A message rings true when it is expressed in the sender's own true voice. Many people reserve their use of the word *love* and other terms of endearment for their romantic relationships or their immediate family members. But there are plenty of other words that can convey your positive emotions for others. Some of the terms you could use include *fondness, respect, admiration, affection, gratitude* and *appreciation*. The specific word or words that you choose are less important than the fact that you have taken the time to express your positive feelings for the other person in your message.

Element 3: What Makes You Special to Me?

Answering element 3's question is a particularly important part of any message that you hope will be a lasting gift for others. To use this element effectively, all you need to do is describe a positive trait that you have observed in the other person. Write one or two sentences about a wonderful characteristic you have noticed that sets this person apart and makes her special, unique and important to you.

Incorporating element 3 into your message is easy. The words you use can be as simple as "I've seen how gentle you are with your little brother, and I like that about you."

Let's take a look at the different versions of Nancy's letter.

Here is her first draft without using the elements:

> I signed you up to take Driver's Ed at school when you get home.

When Carrie read this, she was annoyed. "I can't believe you'd do that without asking me," she sputtered at her mother. "I wanted to pick the class myself so I could be in the same one as my friends!"

Now, notice the feelings that come up in you as you read her good and even better drafts.

This is her good version:

> One of the things I like best about you is the way you plan ahead and take care of things. So, when your school called to ask if you wanted to take Driver's Ed in the fall, I said I thought you would. They're holding a spot in the lunchtime class.
> Write to me soon and let me know if that's what you want. OK?

Carrie reacted to this version more calmly. She looked up at her mother and said, "Well, that's better."

And here is Nancy's even better version:

> I'm so impressed by the way you take care of things that need doing. (When I hear other parents complain that their kids put things off to the last minute, I realize just how terrific you are.) Anyway, your school called me today and said they had one spot left in the lunchtime Driver's Ed class this fall and did I think you'd want it. I said yes. I hope that was all right. If not, we'll change things around when you get home. OK?

Carrie grinned when she read this version. "I didn't know you even noticed that I'm good at taking care of details like that," she said softly. "It's probably a good thing you held that spot open for me. Thanks."

When you put your positive observations about others in your message, you help the receivers

- ◆ feel appreciated
- ◆ sense their significance to you

- know you are glad they are in your life (this can be especially meaningful to people who may wonder if you'd value them if they weren't a family relative)
- feel more open to absorbing the contents of your messages—even if you are writing about uncomfortable or upsetting events

Tip for Using Element 3: What Makes You Special to Me?

How can I use this element in a letter to someone when things are shaky between us?

When your relationship is rocky, using this element can really help because it lets the other person know that despite the problems between you, you continue to value your connection to him. And, while this may be a difficult thing to do, if what the two of you have together is important to you, applying element 3 is well worth the effort. Here's a good example to show you how this works:

> Last time we got together, things didn't go too well. But I've always admired your willingness to hang in there without giving up. So I would like to keep trying to fix things between us.

This example is a good beginning. The receiver is likely to want to read on. But what's missing and what would make this a stronger and more effective letter is a clear statement about the specific things the sender values in the other person. That's what the sender added to the words in this even better example:

> Last time we got together, things didn't go too well. But I admire your willingness to hang in there even when things are tense. You've shown me that working through tough times can actually strengthen a relationship. So, now that's what I want to do, too. I don't want to give up without trying to fix things between us.

Element 4:
What Do I Remember and Treasure About Our Time Together?

When someone receives a message from you that includes the details of an event the two of you shared, she feels important and has a greater sense of how much you value her. Why else, she wonders, would you still be able to recall a time you shared? The more fully you fill in the details about what you remember, the more fully the other person will be able to pull up her own memories and reexperience her relationship to you.

The key to using this element most effectively is to look back and describe a shared experience (happy or sad) that left you feeling more connected to the other person. We think that Nancy used the *What do I remember and treasure about our time together?* element effectively in her good and in her even better drafts.

Here is her good version:

> Carrie, remember when I took you to your friend Sarah's
> birthday party but it turned out that her party wasn't
> until the next day?

And here is her even better version:

> Carrie, remember when I took you to your friend Sarah's
> birthday party but it turned out that her party wasn't until
> the next day? I still giggle about how, after that happened,
> you introduced me to Sarah as your mother, Mrs. Early
> Bird! I love your quick wit and your sense of humor.

What makes this version even better is fairly obvious. Nancy added more details about the event that she remembered and shared her positive reaction to it with the words "I still giggle." And when Carrie read this section of her mom's letter, she laughed out loud.

Although Nancy drew on a delightful shared memory to apply this element in her letter to Carrie, we want to make sure that we address one more important point about the *What do I remember and treasure about our time together?* element. The memory that you describe when you use element 4 can be a small, gentle moment, such as watching your child play with his first puppy, or a more dramatic and uncomfortable situation, such as sitting with a friend whose spouse is dying. It does not matter whether you write about a positive or negative experience that the two of you have shared. What matters is that you draw upon your recollection of a time that strengthened your relationship to the other person. Answering *What do I remember and treasure about our time together?* in your message helps the receiver

- know that your shared history holds special meaning for you
- pull up her own recollections of your shared past
- feel appreciated by you even if you haven't seen each other in a long time

Tip for Using Element 4:
What Do I Remember and Treasure About Our Time Together?

How do I use this element if I'm writing to a person I barely know or to someone I haven't even met yet?

This question might occur to you if you are writing to

- ✦ people you will be meeting soon (your future in-laws, for example)
- ✦ someone who is facing a situation similar to one you have experienced (maybe an acquaintance lost his job and you've gone through that, too)
- ✦ those who haven't even been born (perhaps generations yet to come will read a note you attach to your family tree)

In cases such as these, there is a variation to element 4 that can help you connect with the other person. Instead of answering, *What do I remember and treasure about our time together?* replace that question with this one: What do we have in common? Answering that question calls for you to briefly describe the beliefs, traditions or experiences that you and the receiver have in common.

Your answers can be as simple as this:

> Thank you for raising a wonderful son. Just like you, I love him very much....

> I heard you've been laid off at work and I've been through that myself, so...

> Dear family, hello from the twentieth century. Boy, have we got a wild history....

When you use this variation of element 4, even people you barely know will be able to sense a bond with you.

Element 5: What Do I Want You to Get From My Message?

Element 5 is your opportunity to add the final touches to your message. When you apply the *What do I want you to get from my message?* element, you tell a person about the thoughts and feelings that you hope he will come away with after reading your words.

The more explicitly you explain the reaction you hope he will have by the time he gets to the end of your message, the more likely it is that he will, in fact, get what you want him to.

Using this element effectively calls for you to
- look back over all that you have written
- spend a few moments thinking about the receiver(s)
- decide what thoughts and feelings you want to leave him with

Maybe you hope that your message will leave him feeling delighted, or motivated to try something new, or perhaps relieved. Ask yourself this: If the other person gets only one thing out of reading my message, what do I hope that will be? Picture the outcome you would like, and then put your hopes for the other person on paper.

Here is how Nancy first applied element 5:

> I hope that when you finish reading this letter you will
> know that I think you're the best daughter in the world.

That is a good summary of the message she created for her daughter. But when Nancy added in more specific information about what she hoped Carrie would get from her message in the long run, she created this even better version:

> I hope that when you finish reading this letter you will know
> that I think you're the best daughter in the world. And I also
> want you to know that, while this summer is the first time
> you've been away for so long, I am so glad that you are having
> a good time. That tells me that someday soon when you're
> grown and out there in the world on your own, you will soar!

When Carrie read her mother's words, her eyes filled with tears. Then she folded her mother's letter carefully and put it into her pocket. A few moments later, Carrie told us that she was going to put her mom's letter in her scrapbook along with all the other mementos she'd been keeping since she was old enough to cut and paste. Here's what happens when you apply element 5:
- you free the other person from having to guess and possibly misinterpret your reasons for writing
- your positive thoughts and feelings for the receiver shine through

Tip for Using Element 5:
What Do I Want You to Get From My Message?

Suppose I'm sending a message to wish someone a happy birthday. What do I put down as my answer to the question in element 5?

When your intention is to wish someone a happy birthday, using this element in a message is a great way to add something to your message that will, in fact, help her enjoy her special day. Reread the words you've already written, spend a few moments thinking about the reaction you'd like your message to produce in the other person, then add a sentence or two that might leave her with a smile. You don't need to write something long or drawn out. Using this element in a birthday greeting might be as short and simple as this:

> So, my friend, I'm sending you this card because I really do want you to have a wonderful birthday. I am picturing you as you are reading this silly card and hoping that you are grinning because you know that I am thinking warm and fuzzy wishes for you.

More About Using the Basic Elements

Now that you know what the five basic elements are and how to use them to create messages that offer lasting meaning and value for others, here are some other brief points we'd like to go over with you.

The order in which you can add these elements to your message is not fixed in stone. But, when we were starting out, many of us found that it was easier to make our messages by applying the elements one at a time in the order in which we have presented them to you here.

You can use each element more than once in your messages. As a matter of fact, several examples in this book use some of the elements more than once in the same message. That's fine. What matters most and will help you to make your words clear and dear to others is your use of all five elements at least once in a message.

Whether you plan to send them now or in the future, put the date on all of your messages. Doing that adds something important: context. Adding context helps people who may read your words in the years to come know how long ago you wrote, how old you were back then and what events might have been going on in your life (and theirs) at the time.

The five basic elements presented here apply to all kinds of lasting messages. However, there are some other special elements you can use to make specific kinds of messages fuller, more personal and more meaningful. We'll look at these special elements when we get to the chapters about repairing relationships, giving advice, revealing secrets and offering comfort.

What You Will Find in the Next Chapter

Now that you have seen how adding the five basic elements to your messages can help you express yourself clearly and with impact, we're going to show you some techniques that can help make creating messages a comfortable, easy and enjoyable thing to do—whether you are a reluctant writer or not.

Two Techniques

$\mathcal{W}$orking on our messages and helping others do this, too, we came upon two techniques that make it easier to move ahead even when you feel insecure about your ability to write or you have mixed feelings about the person you're writing to.

Putting Your Purpose on Paper

Here is a straightforward and easy technique that can help you make certain your message will reflect your genuine and positive intentions. Just write down what you want someone to get from your letter. Keep it short and simple. "Putting your purpose on paper" in just a few words before you create your message is particularly helpful when your message
- is about something that is difficult for you to discuss
- may be unpleasant for the receiver to learn about
- runs the risk of being manipulative or self-serving

To demonstrate how putting your purpose on paper helps you stay on course, our friend "John" agreed to let us show you how he put his purpose on paper and then developed a message. John wanted to write to his son, "David," who, like many teenagers, was angry about the limits his parents set for him. Lately, David had been particularly argumentative.

We chose to show you this letter because the technique and approach will work well whether you are writing to a spouse, a friend, an older person or anyone else for that matter.

This is how John put his purpose on paper. On a sheet of paper, he completed the following sentence in his own words. We asked him to keep what he wrote here simple and short.

_____ The gift I want to give you in this message: _____
_____ Something that helped me understand my parents _____
_____ when I was in the same boat you are in now. _____

Then, John wrote his first draft to David using the five basic elements. (To help you see what makes each message work, we've marked where each element is being used, e.g. [1] designates when the first element, *What got me thinking about you?* is being used.)

Here is John's first draft:

April 4, 1996
Dear David,
This morning when you complained that I "always side with Mom," you were hollering so much that nothing I could say was going to get through. [1] So, I want you to calm down before you read this. I love you [2] but you sure know how to aggravate me. Still, one of the things that I like best about you is the way you always let me know how you feel. [3] In fact, I remember when you were seven years old and you were thinking about running away from home. Remember that? [4] Just before you headed out the door, you came and told me what was bothering you—and we worked it out. I was so glad you did that! So knowing that we can always talk things out, I am going to respond to your complaint about me and Mom.

When it comes to deciding what's best for you, it's nowhere near as easy as it looks. In order to reach an agreement, your mom and I do a lot of talking first (actually, sometimes what we do is a lot louder than talking), and we keep at it until we can come up with a decision that feels right to both of us. We try to be fair with each other and you.

Your grandfather told me that he did things this way when I complained about the same thing to him (but not as obnoxiously as you). What he told me back then helped me understand my parents and it taught me how to be as good a father as I can to my own children, and that's what I hope you'll get from this letter. [5] Years ago, he said, "Son, if I am a good father to you now *and* a good partner to your mother, then, when you grow up and head out on your own, I'll be able to stay right here and go on living with your mom!"

Love,
Dad

Then, John reread the purpose he had put on paper and compared it to the actual contents of his message. We asked him (and suggest that you do this, too) to watch out for words that sounded as if he were being critical, blaming or sarcastic; ordering David around; trying to manipulate him; or seeking self-pity. When John found words and themes that didn't match his written purpose (and almost everyone does), we told him just to scratch them out.

Below you can see the words that John crossed out before he made his final draft of this letter for David:

April 4, 1996
Dear David,
This morning when you complained that I "always side with Mom," ~~you were hollering so much that nothing I could say was going to get through. So, I want you to calm down before you read this~~. I love you ~~but you sure know how to aggravate me~~. Still, one of the things that I like best about you is the way you always let me (and I hope other people that you are close to) know how you feel. In fact, I remember when you were seven years old and you were thinking about running away from home. Remember that? Just before you headed out the door, you came and told me what was bothering you—and we worked it out. I was so glad you did that! So knowing that we can always talk things out, I am going to respond to your complaint about me and Mom.

When it comes to deciding what's best for you, it's nowhere near as easy as it looks. In order to reach an agreement, your mom and I do a lot of talking first (actually, sometimes what we do is a lot louder than talking), and we keep at it until we can come up with a decision that feels right to both of us. We try to be fair with each other and you.

Your grandfather told me that he did things this way when I complained about the same thing to him ~~(but not~~

~~as obnoxiously as you did~~). What he told me back then helped me understand my parents and it taught me how to be as good a father as I can to my own children, and that's what I hope you'll get from this letter. Years ago, he said, "Son, if I am a good father to you now *and* a good partner to your mother, then, when you grow up and head out on your own, I'll be able to stay right here and go on living with your mom!"

Love, Dad

John explained that the words he had scratched out were the ones that made him sound angry and blaming:

Even though I was angry, I knew that if I left those words in it would only make David feel defensive. Since all I really wanted was for him to get what I was saying without adding more fuel to the fire, I figured I'd do better to take out anything that might get in the way of his being able to hear me.

Now take a look at John's final draft, in which he omitted the words that did not conform to his positive intentions. John also added a delightful sentence at the end of his letter. We think his final version is a lasting message that sparkles with personality, wisdom and gentle good humor. See for yourself:

April 4, 1996
Dear David,
This morning when you complained that I "always side with Mom," I was glad to hear that you think your mother and I always agree. [1] I love you very much [2], and one of the things I like best about you is the way you let me (and I hope other people that you are close to) know how you feel about things. [3 and 4] So I thought I'd try and respond to your complaint.

When it comes to deciding what's best for you, it's nowhere near as easy as it looks. In order to reach an agreement, your mom and I do a lot of talking first (actually, sometimes what we do is a lot louder than talking), and we keep at it until we can come up with a decision that feels right to both of us. We try to be fair with each other and you.

Your grandfather told me that he did things this way, when I complained about the same thing to him. What he told me back then helped me understand my parents and it also taught me how to be as good a father as I can to my own children, and that's what I hope you'll get from my message, too. [5] Years ago, he said, "Son, if I am a good father to you now *and* a good partner to your mother, then, when you grow up and head out on your own, I'll be able to stay right here and go on living with your mom!"

David, I've followed my father's example and you know what? So far, it seems to be working.

Love,

Dad

Putting your purpose on paper is just that simple. The more closely you look over your message to make sure it conforms with your wish to get through and help someone else, the more likely it is that the receiver will find value in what you are sharing.

And just like John, it may take you several drafts to line up the contents of your message with your purpose. But when you do this, you are much more likely to end up with a finished message that really is a gift.

Writing in the Margins

"Writing in the margins" simply involves jotting down in the margins your worries, fears, assumptions, anger, regrets and any other uncomfortable or distracting feelings that get in your way when you sit down to create a message. No matter how easy or difficult the things you are trying to express in your message may be, this technique helps you make sure that the words that go into the body of your completed message will be those that are most likely to feel like a gift to the other person.

You can use this technique to draft any kind of message. In most cases, your final draft will not include the words you write in the margins; these generally are intended to be notes to yourself.

Writing in the margins helps you notice and track your inner thoughts and feelings—without letting them get in your way. It gives you a safe place to lay out all your thoughts and feelings (good, bad and ugly), even the ones that are blaming, denying, justifying or pretending. And there are times when it helps you notice some assumptions you may have made about what the other person thinks or feels so you can ask questions and get more information from him.

To show you how writing in the margins helps you stay on course, below is a letter from a woman named "Amy" to her husband, "Fred." Growing up,

Amy hated writing assignments. Even now she was worried about her spelling, use of grammar and penmanship. Reluctantly, she agreed to try writing this letter strictly to help us fine-tune some of our message-making suggestions.

Amy was so uncomfortable with the idea of writing anything that we asked her to jot down (in the right-hand margin) what she was thinking and feeling as she went along. We hoped that would help Amy look at and then let go of her discomfort. And it worked. By writing in the margins, Amy was able to put her worries and thoughts aside (literally) so that by the time she got to the end of her letter, she actually felt connected to the truth of her own words.

What She Wrote:	**What She Was Thinking:**

November 16, 1998
Dear Fred,
The only reason I am writing this is to see if I can make you understand how I feel with words on paper because my friends from the coffee shop asked me to do this. [1]

I hate writing.
Why did I say I'd try this?

This is so dumb.

I don't do much writing about my feelings or anything else. I do better just talking, and besides, you already know I love you. [2]

He already knows I love him—
we've been together since the ninth
grade for crying out loud.
Blah, blah, blah.

You are the most special person in my life because you are steady and you don't hide things from me and so I can feel like you trust me and that makes me proud. [3]

Well, at least he's better than my
friend's husband, who lies to her all
the time.

We sure have been through a lot together. Like when Jimmy was in the hospital and we didn't know if he would ever get well. We spent so much time praying in the hospital, remember? You held my hand the whole time and I liked that. [4]

Other men would have run out.
Thank God Fred didn't.

I wrote this just to see if I could, but now I want to keep going and thank you for being the best person I ever met.

When I was writing about when Jimmy was sick, I remembered other

I'd forgotten a
lot of this.

things like how you hate to have your picture taken but you do it for me anyway and how safe I feel when you hug me.

Well, I don't want you to get a swelled head from this, but I do want you to know that after all the years we have been together, I am happy that you are my friend and my husband! [5]

Love,
Amy

I really do love Fred a lot.

When Amy finished her letter, she slowly looked back over her words and seemed stunned. "I can't believe I wrote that," she said with a huge sigh of relief. Then she told us she was going to redo her letter, leaving her margin notes out so that she could give it to her husband, Fred. "He just won't believe this! I mean Fred knows that school was so awful for me that I've never written anything since I got out of there, well, except for grocery lists. I bet his jaw drops when he reads what I wrote here!"

Many people told us they were just as surprised to find that by writing in the margins they could dump their distracting, unkind or unpleasant feelings, let go of their worries about writing and their concerns about the other person's reaction and get on with creating their messages.

Where Do You Go From Here?

At this point, you've read about the basic elements and techniques that can make creating your messages deeply meaningful and surprisingly easy, and now you are ready to settle back and read through the rest of this book. Each of the next chapters deals with a specific kind of message, ranging from expressions of love to giving advice or offering comfort.

To help you keep the elements and techniques clearly in mind, in each chapter we will look closely at one or more messages where the sender(s) applied the elements and techniques in especially effective ways. In some chapters, you'll find additional techniques that will help you with specific types of messages.

Feel free to go directly to the chapters that speak to you. Or, just read from here on out, letting all the messages inspire you, no matter what your message-writing occasion may be.

4

Messages for Friends and Siblings

$\mathcal{W}$hen you are thinking about making your messages, sometimes it's easy to overlook the people who are closest to you—your friends and siblings. In this chapter, you'll see what happened when several people took the time to acknowledge their close friends and siblings with love and thanks. Their messages range from chatty letters to briefer greeting card messages, lengthy lists, a handwritten note attached to a cartoon and even some lighthearted verses of poetry.

Each message incorporates the five basic elements. And each one shows you a different, effective, easy and everyday way to express your love and appreciation in a lasting message. We hope that as you read these, you will find yourself thinking about your own friends and siblings and that a number of these different messages will spark your enthusiasm.

❥ *Her Newly Wedded Friend*

The letter below communicates warmth and welcome to someone who is facing the kind of difficulties that often confront people who "marry into" a close-knit group of friends.

As you read this wonderful letter, notice the order in which the sender applies the basic elements. She uses all five but not in the same order as we laid them out for you in chapter two. And yet, what she does works well! We wanted to show you this to make the point—once again—that what matters is that you use all five elements in your messages; what doesn't matter is the order in which you apply them.

What She Wrote:

What She Was Thinking:

December 12, 1998
Dear Sherry,
In a few weeks, you and I (and our husbands) will be vacationing together. I was thinking about that and about how hard it must be for you to have "married" into a group of friends with such a long history. [1] Years ago, I remember feeling like the "lone Yankee" among all the friends my husband had grown up with. I remember having to listen to stories about past experiences they'd shared, inside jokes that left me out and endless details about a history that predated me. There were lots of times that I felt sad, frustrated and more than a little pissed! I don't know if that is how you are feeling or not. But if you are, I want you to know that I've watched you quietly carve a space for yourself in our midst and I am grateful for your efforts to connect with me. You bring a wonderful balance to the times that the four of us share. [2]

Since you've come into our lives, my husband has had someone to shop with, talk gardening with or just plop down to watch TV with. And I have had someone to commiserate with about "womany things," like weight gain, wrinkles and hot flashes. I love that you are willing to explore "humany things" with me, too, like what we really want to do with our lives and how to balance what we want in the face of other people's expectations. [4]

The wonderful gifts you have brought into your husband's life are clear to us. He loves being married to you and it shows! You've added a

I'm worried that she doesn't think I like her.

If I were Sherry, this is the kind of letter I'd want, but what if it's too touchy-feely for her?

My husband's friends made it really hard for me to feel like I had a right to be there with them.

Back then it felt awful.

I think Sherry is the best thing that has happened to her husband and our group of friends in a long time.

It's amazing the way she fits into our group and makes all of us glad she's here—and I guess she doesn't even know that I've noticed this stuff.

Her husband must be feeling good about himself. He even walks differently—now he sort of struts.

sense of purpose to his life that I think has made him an even more remarkable, fully alive man.

I want you to know that for me, your quiet presence in our lives is a valuable present! [3]

Most of our day in, day out communicating with one another happens indirectly, so, I wanted to make sure that, at least this one time, I told you directly how glad I am that you are my "newly wedded" friend. [5]

I don't want her to think I am pushy, but it is stupid for me to always go through her husband when I have something to tell her.

❧ *A Few of Her Favorite Things*

Some people find it easier to make lists than to write in complete sentences. If that sounds like you, then here is an example that shows you how to make a message powerful and clear simply by listing your thoughts and feelings:

> August 1997
> Dear Michael,
> This is definitely not a good-bye letter. But I was sitting here remembering how you once told me you'd be afraid to live on without me. [1] I felt worried and so I decided to write to you because, even though I plan on being around for a long time, what if something happened? I want you to have this letter to help you miss me with a smile and make it easy for you to keep on being the obnoxious, in-your-face, delightful and absolutely grand man you are. [5]
>
> I'm not sure how to sum up the ways you've touched my life, so I divided my thoughts and feelings into categories. I'll probably be adding to this letter forever. It's a gift in progress because that's what you are to me.
>
> My thank-yous [4]:
> 1. Thanks for listening to me and hearing me so fully.
> 2. Thanks for your unconditional love—the most remarkable I've ever known.
> 3. Thanks for staying connected to me on a day in, day out basis.
> 4. Thanks for trusting me with your truths.
> 5. Thanks for loving me no matter what size I am.
> 6. Thanks for letting me give you so many of my "hum-

ble" opinions.

7. Thanks for telling me the truth even when it was embarrassing.
8. Thanks for not judging me and for leaving me lots of room to change my mind.
9. Thanks for sticking your tongue in my mouth at my party—it's left me with a photo that makes me laugh.
10. Thanks for smoothing my way so many times.
11. Thanks for letting me refuse your phone calls and never taking it personally.

Here's a list of my favorite things about you [3]:

1. When you decide to do something (learn to ski, go into therapy or get married), you bring every bit of your energy, focus and laughter into the process.
2. You are always ready to be honest with yourself (and me!).
3. You like to take charge and you do it so well.
4. You're allergic to our cat but you visit us anyway.
5. You earned your way into my children's lives and hearts.
6. You found a way to be my best friend and my husband's (a tricky balancing act for sure!).
7. You always wear comfortable clothes, fashion be damned!
8. You love new adventures.
9. You promise not to chew food with your mouth open when you are old.
10. You don't like to go shopping, either.
11. You always make time for me if I need you.
12. You love me.

This is a list of the things we learned together. I'm leaving them with you because nobody I know will use them better! And I want you to pass them along to other people:

1. Gut-wrenching self-honesty followed by laughter
2. Forgiveness of ourselves when we screw up

Here's what you gave me:

1. An appreciation of how important it is to stay in touch with one another over the little things that happen not just the big events that mark our lives
2. An ability to like the part of me that shook free of the

"I should" to find the "I want" in my life
Here's what I gave you:
  Complete permission to be as real as possible

And this is what is absolutely true:
  God, how you are loved. [2]

❧ Secrets and Laughter

This message makes the point that there are times when adding a few personal words to a preprinted greeting card captures a shared moment perfectly. When a friend of ours received the card below, she went out of her way to show it to us because she was certain that it met all the requirements of a special message. We agreed. Here is how our friend described the card she received and her reaction to it:

A few days after I'd shared secret truths (the kind that are hard for me to talk about) with one of my best girlfriends, I got this card in the mail from her. On the cover was a cartoon of a frazzled, stick-figure woman who was about to explode. The card's printed words made me burst out laughing!
The outside of the card said:
  In Margaret's day, women didn't have all of this "Take-it-one-day-at-a-time-be-your-own-best-friend-and-go-easy-on-yourself" stuff. Women buckled down, accepted what they got, and never talked about what they wanted.

Inside the card, it read:
  Margaret is now serving a life sentence at the Olive Trotter Asylum for Women Who Crack Walnuts With Their Sphincter.

My friend added these words:

December 29, 1997
Thanks for trusting me with all that is going on in your life right now. [1] You make me feel special [2]—I think that might be one of my favorite things about you, but I'm not sure because there are so many other things that make you a great friend. [3] Anyway I'm glad we can talk, laugh and cry together. Remember the "bad old days" when we didn't even like each other? [4] Glad we got over all that stuff. If not, we'd probably be cracking walnuts in adjoining straightjackets now! I want you to know that our friendship is very special to me. [5]

We knew this message was a "keeper" when our friend said, "Whenever I look at this card, it always makes me smile."

❧ *Cheesecake for Her "Inner Child"*

A young man we met at our neighborhood coffee shop showed us a cartoon featuring a character raiding a refrigerator for cheesecake. He also showed us the note he attached to it to cheer up a friend. We think it's a great example of how passing along cartoons or other newspaper clippings with explanations about how they delighted or taught you something can be an easy way to create special messages that really get through to others.

And better still—if you are reluctant to write, you'll be pleased to know that this message applies all five elements in less than one hundred words.

Here is the note he attached to the cartoon:

> April 12, 1999
> When I saw this cartoon in the morning paper, it
> made me laugh so hard I spilled coffee all over my-
> self. It reminded me of how both of us tend to turn
> to the contents of our refrigerators for comfort. [1]
> You have always been there for me when I'm having
> a problem [3 and 4], so even though you live too far
> away for me to come over and eat you out of house
> and home, I hope this will bring a chuckle your way.
> I know you are going through a tough time, and I
> wanted you to know that I care and miss hearing
> from you. [2 and 5]
> > Love,
> > John

In the note that he attached to this cartoon, "John" used a single sentence to combine two elements. His words "I wanted you to know that I care and miss hearing from you" pull together elements 2, *What are my positive feelings for you?* and 5, *What do I want you to get from my message?* Again, we want to make this point: As long as you include all five elements in your messages, neither the order in which you use them nor the way in which you combine them will affect the impact of your words.

❧ *Getting Back to Business*

This is a fairly long letter that was sent by a woman named "Margaret" to her best friend, "Deborah." The letter deals with the kinds of problems women face if they have been home for years raising their families and then later want to reenter the job market. Notice the way Margaret wrote using her true voice and the caring way she shared her feelings, supported her friend and offered practical advice. And yes, we'd like you to notice that she used all five basic elements in her message. Here it is:

> September 1999
> Dear Deborah,
> I just got off the phone with you. I could tell from the sound of your voice that you're pretty stressed out about being able to get back to the kind of work you used to do. [1] Do you remember when I told you that I felt the same way when I wanted to get my old job back after being a full-time stay-at-home mom for nineteen years? It took me over a year to get up the nerve to try to convince someone to hire me.
>
> OK, so it ain't easy, but it can be done. If I could do it, then you, my friend with more guts and brains than anyone else I've ever met [3], can get back on that horse and ride off to conquer anything you want.
>
> I believe that about you today as much as I did a hundred years ago when we were two hicks setting out to make our way in the big, bad city. [4]
>
> I do not have any great advice to give you, just one idea that worked for me. Here's what I did. I put copies of my resume in clear-plastic photo cubes and hand delivered them to the secretaries of everyone I could think of.
>
> Maybe, since you're interested in working in an advertising firm where creativity is appreciated, this kind of approach will help you, too. The man who hired me said I just wore him down because my resume was too clunky to fit in a file cabinet like everyone else's. So it sat there on his desk for weeks until he finally called me to come in for an interview.
>
> Here's how I made my resume. The top panel had a color photo of me with tracing paper over it where I typed my name, address, phone number and a sentence about what kind of position I was looking for. On each of the four side panels, I put information like this:
>
> Educational Background:
>
> Besides the usual school stuff, I added in every convention or workshop I ever attended. I ended up with a surprisingly good list of things.
>
> Work Experience:
>
> Along with a list of the jobs I'd held before the kids came along, I wrote about running scout meetings and

Little League scheduling and described it like the impressive logistics feat that it was.

Who Else Knows Me:

This is where I put the names and phone numbers of businesspeople I'd asked to put in a good word for me. These included folks I'd met when I was a soccer mom, etc. All those years of being friendly to everybody really paid off in this respect because I had some really good references.

What I Want to Do Now:

I changed what I wrote on this panel on each one of my photo-cube resumes so that the typed info here matched up with whatever I knew about the company I was giving it to.

Whether you use this idea or come up with something completely different, believe this: Any agency that hires you will be getting a bargain in talent, energy and brains. [5] So, go get 'em pal and keep me posted. OK?

I love you [2],

Margaret

❧ Brother Dear, It's Your Turn

A gift given twice may mean different things at different times. The messages we get and save seem to take on greater meaning when we add our own words to them before passing them along.

In this example, a man added value to an old message before passing it on. He brought back to life the words that his eighteen-year old sister had written to him three decades earlier.

Here is how his sister described what happened:

Thirty-two years ago, I bought a thick, phone book–size manual that was pretty much the bible for anyone applying to college. It had all the information you could possibly need about every college and university in America.

I'll bet I lugged that book around with me everywhere I went for months. Then, when I finally got accepted by my "first choice" school, I wrote a poem on the inside cover of the book and officially presented it to my younger brother who was next in line to apply for college. Here's what I wrote:

November 1964
Brother dear, look here, look here,
For schools both far and near.
This book has been quite handy,

Its contents were just dandy.
And now it's yours, my brother dear,
It's up to you—I'm out of here!

I'd forgotten all about this nonsense until thirty-two years later when my brother stopped by with that old book and gave it to my son who had just begun applying to colleges. On the inside cover, underneath the poem I'd written, my brother had added these words:

October 1996
Dear nephew of mine (son of sister so fine),
The years have flown by,
From the coop you must fly.
Though this book may be old,
Here's what is true,
While college is great, it's all up to you!

And my brother also wrote this note to my son:

Dear Jake,
Your mom told me about your latest report card and man was I impressed! [1] Way to go! I am proud of you. [5]. But that's no surprise. I still remember the time you stood up for your sister against bullies who were calling her bad names. [4] Took a lot of guts. [3] I like that about you. You get that from your mom. She's a gutsy lady, too. Jake, you are a great kid and now you are on your way to being a great man. I love you [2],
Uncle George

My son loved the note his uncle wrote and the old college book, too! And now I think he is planning to write something in that book so he can give it to his younger sister because she'll be applying to schools herself pretty soon.

❥ *Little Big Sister*

In the message below, which is from an adult woman to her older sister, we want you to notice the way in which the sender recalls a painful and difficult time that, for her own private reasons, she chose not to detail. Instead, she applied element 4 (*What do I remember and treasure about our time together?*) with the words "If not for your love, understanding and strength, I might not be here at all today" and powerfully connected the two women with their shared history. The younger sister told us this:

I have a sister who is different from me in every way. She's five years older and several inches shorter. I'm a redhead (natural) and she's a brunette (used to be natural). Years ago, my sister helped me get through a really tough time. This is the note I wrote inside a card that I gave her back then:

> 2/19/83
> I just looked at the calendar and when I saw that it has been exactly one and a half years since I arrived in the same city as you, I almost gasped in surprise. [1] You know, when I first came here, I really was afraid that living so close was going to be bad for both of us. You showed me how wrong a girl can be! If not for your love, understanding and strength [3], I might not be here at all today. [4] I want you to know that I love you little big sister. [2 and 5]

❧ The Neatest Shawl of All

"Anna," a woman in her late forties, sparkles with joy whenever she wears the cream-colored shawl that her brother gave her more than twenty years ago. She said:

> *I love the fact that he "tricked" me into telling him exactly what I would like as a gift. Then he went out and bought it for me and even told me how much he cares about me in the note he put in the gift box that contained this shawl.*

And we were particularly pleased to notice that Anna's brother instinctively used all five basic elements. In fact, in the very first sentence, the words "I want you to know what a help you are and always have been to me" are a straightforward application of element 5, *What do I want you to get from my message?* Here is how Anna described her experience:

> *My brother and I have always been close. But he did something for me once that really touched my heart. I'd been helping him fill out applications for medical school and running a few errands for him while he worked two jobs and finished up his last three undergrad classes at college. No big deal. I had the time and I wanted to help him. A few days after he'd been accepted to medical school, he phoned me and said he needed advice. He wanted to know what he could give to a woman he cared about. I asked if this was a romantic gift and he said no, so I told him that a soft knit shawl would be nice. The next day, I found a gift box outside my door with this shawl and this note:*

May 6, 1974
Dear Anna,
I want you to know what a help you are and always have
been to me. [5] I don't know what I would have done if you
hadn't been the kind of energetic and organized person
you are. [3] Now that the worst is over, I can take time to
tell you how good it is to have you on my side. [1] I hope
this shawl is what you would have picked out if you'd gone
to the store yourself, because you are exactly the sister I
would have picked if Mom and Dad had given me a
choice! Thanks for helping me hold it together these last
few months. [4] I really am grateful. [2]
    Love,
    N.

*I opened the box and found this gorgeous shawl. Every time I wear it, I feel
special because I know that my brother appreciates me. Pretty neat, huh?*

5

For the Love of Our Children

$\mathcal{C}$reating loving messages for our children is a special joy. And holding onto the things we make for them helps us track their growth (and ours) over time. That way, when our children are grown, the messages we've saved for them can be passed along again as gifts that are likely to be treasured and cherished for years to come.

❧ *Two Hands Full*

Here is a handmade birthday card from a mother to her ten-year-old daughter. We think it shows that you don't have to be a writer or an artist to make wonderful lasting messages. This card is a marvelous gift in itself, and if the little girl's parents hold onto it for her now and return it to their daughter when she's grown, it may take on even more meaning the second time around.

We particularly liked the way the sender applied all five basic elements in her message. She spread them out—some are included at the top of her card, and others are written right into the card's design as phrases on the fingers of the hands she traced.

Here are the words this woman wrote at the top of her card:

> February 10, 1992
> Dear Emily,
> Because you are ten years old today [1], I traced your
> hands, and on each of your fingers, I wrote about some-
> thing you already have that makes you very special. I hope

you will hold onto these special gifts of yours forever. [5] I love being your mother and I love you. [2]

XXXXOOOOOXXXX,

Mommy

You are small but very strong.

You have a gentle touch. Remember all those back rubs you gave us? We do, and we love them and you.

You know how to protect yourself from danger– you're awesome at karate.

You are willing to reach out and help others, like the children you visit in the hospital.

You have the gift of a green thumb.

The comments written on each finger show you an unusual and effective way to use elements 3 and 4.

You hold tight to things that are really important in life.

You push me to be the best mom I can be.

You know that you hold your own destiny in your hands.

You write wonderful stories that we like to read.

You like to try new things, and you enjoy learning.

❧ *The Truth Fairy*

This message is an example of how, simply by adding a new message to an old one, your words can take on deeper meaning and offer something of lasting value to other people.

In this instance, a friend of ours who has an eighteen-year-old daughter took an old message and attached a new note to her original one. Here is the wonderful story she told us:

The other day, I found this note stuck way in the back of my top dresser drawer. I laughed out loud when I read what I'd written eleven years ago, just after my seven-year-old daughter told me in a sad, little voice that the tooth she'd lost the day before was still under her pillow. I felt so guilty about forgetting to play "tooth fairy" that the next night I scribbled and then shoved this note underneath my daughter's pillow:

> September 11, 1987
> Dear Tooth Fairy,
> You need to pay double for this tooth because you were late!
>> Thank you very much,
>> Rachel's Mommy

I am going to put this note away carefully, and someday, when my daughter is a mother herself, I'll give it back to her with this other note that I wrote to her:

> September 1998
> Rachel, when I was cleaning out my dresser drawers today, I found this old note that I made for you when you were still young enough to believe in tooth fairies. [1] I read it, sat down on my bed and laughed to myself. Remember how much each tooth fairy visit meant to you back then? [4] You used to poke your little fingers around inside your mouth and wiggle each tooth hoping you could loosen it so the tooth fairy would come back to see you even sooner. Come to think of it, you've always believed that you could make things happen and I love that about you! [3]
>> Thinking about all that made me decide to write this note to you because I do love you so much. [2]
>> I guess I want you to know that all moms mess up. And when that happens, you pay the price, wipe away some tears and hope you can smile about it in a few years.

But the most important thing you can do when you screw up is to pass what you've learned on to the next generation. [5] That's what I'm trying to do for you with this note.
Love,
Mom (aka your "Tooth Fairy")

❧ *Parents on the Same Page*

There is another kind of written message that those of you who are parents may want to create together. When fathers and mothers express their different and wonderful views of a child jointly, their written words are likely to resonate deeply in their children and be kept for years to come.

Below are birthday messages that parents of a thirteen-year-old daughter wrote inside a jumbo-sized birthday greeting card they bought at a specialty shop in their local mall. You may notice that neither of Leigh's parents come right out and use element 1 (*What got me thinking about you?*) in their messages. That is because, in this case, what prompted them to create messages for their daughter was spelled out clearly on the cover of the greeting card with these words:

Happy Birthday, Daughter,
It's Official
You Are a Teenager!

However, because Leigh's parents are close friends of ours, they knew about the five basic elements and—in their own individual ways and in their own true voices—they made sure their messages included all the other elements.

Here is what they wrote:

From Dad:

May 1998
Dear Leigh,
Funny what thirteen years can do. When you were born, I didn't need glasses to read and I didn't need sunblock on top of my head.

Now, just when I've learned how to deal with my little girl, she becomes a young woman and no one gave me a rule book. But you were the girl and you are the young woman I love and respect. I admire

From Mom:

May 1998
Dear Leigh,
You are amazing. You are a loveable, wonderful, and completely awesome, filled-with-questions, looking-for-answers kind of person. [3]

And you've always been that way! You are what we call our "trying" child. At two you tried to see what the walls looked like on the other side of the wallpaper. At five you tried to find out how much your tenacity, honesty, compassion and sense of fair play. [3] From taking on the school administration so that girls could play touch football just like the boys, to teaching children to read music, to denying yourself the lead in a play because one of your friends wanted it more, you have always had an extraordinary sense of integrity. [4]

I love that I can learn from you as I teach you. I love that you make me smile. But mostly I love the confidence you have in your beliefs, your goals, your ambition and yourself. [3]

You are a remarkable combination of people. I like to think that God has given you our best traits. From your mother you've inherited beauty, strength and a sense of independence that is both galling and beguiling. From your grandparents, you received talent and creativity; from your great-grandmothers, grace and charm; and from me, an enjoyment of sports, an argumentative nature and the hair I wish I could've kept.

This moment is bittersweet. It's time to say good-bye to the little girl who says her prayers with me each night, and welcome the young woman who fills me with pride and happiness each day. [5]

I love you [2],
Dad

paper could be stuffed into a toilet bowl before it would overflow. At eight you made birthday cakes with popcorn frosting. At nine you convinced your ballet teacher to let you sing a duet with your grandfather in the middle of your dance recital. [4]

Your creativity is a special joy. You make us smile, even at the end of a long day.

When you leap off the school bus, we are never sure what country you'll be from, what accent you'll be trying or even what age you'll be!

You are the smallest, toughest soccer player in the whole darn town.

You argue creatively by explaining how your mistakes are absolutely, positively and entirely my fault—and then, when that doesn't work, you just burst out laughing!

You believe in yourself and so do we. [5] All I can say is look out world, everyone had better get ready because here comes my trying daughter!

Happy birthday, honey!
I love you very much [2],
Mom

❧ *A Laptop Full of Love*

A client of Paul's, whose oldest child had just left home to go to a college several hundred miles away, showed us a copy of a message that she'd printed out after she put it on her son's new laptop computer. She was especially glad that she had used the basic elements in her message and said doing so had helped her make sure she wrote from the heart and expressed herself clearly. This is what she told us:

I was so emotional about my son leaving home that I held myself tightly in check. I went about helping him unpack his things and set up his dorm room like some sort of unfeeling robot. I just didn't want to cry and embarrass him in front of his roommate. So when I had a minute alone, I grabbed my son's laptop and typed out a quick note on it to him. I left my note in an open file on his computer desktop. I knew he'd see it the next time he used his computer—which I guessed would be after I had kissed him good-bye.

This is what I wrote:

August 1998

Dear Kevin,

I remember the very first time you spent the night away from home. [4] You were seven years old and your cousins took you on a weeklong camping trip. Now, it's eleven years later, you're moving into a college dorm and I feel the way that I did back then. I feel sad about saying good-bye to you and happy that you are about to have new adventures that are all your own.

Before it was even time for Dad and me to kiss you good-bye, I knew that I'd have a hard time holding back my tears. I didn't want to cry and embarrass you in front of your new roommate. So to keep myself in check, I acted stiff and kind of abrupt. I wanted to write this so you'd know that was the reason I acted that way. [1]

You are so special to me—hope you know that you are really going to be missed. [2] Besides being bright and funny and caring, you have always had a love of music. [3] You've even taught your dear old mom to enjoy new kinds of music. I can't wait to see how you grow and pull all your talents together into a career that makes you glad to go to work each day.

I hope that college is a wonderful time for you to grow and have fun for the next four years. I want you to know that I love you and miss you and trust you to follow your head as well as your heart as you meet new people and learn new things. [5] Take care of yourself.

See you at Thanksgiving.

Love,

Mom

6

Parents, Grandparents and Other Grand Folks

*I*n the previous chapter, we looked at loving messages written by parents for their young children. In this chapter, we are focusing on messages created by adult children for their parents, grandparents and other special older people. These are the grand people who have been there guiding and helping all of us throughout our lives.

How many of them would love to receive a written confirmation from you letting them know that what they have done all these years really has made a wonderful difference in your life? Wouldn't it be great to give them the kind of "lift" that an unexpected thank-you can deliver?

As you read through these examples, we'd like you to imagine that you are the recipient so that you can feel and enjoy the reactions that messages like these often produce in others.

✦ *And Suddenly He Understood*

The father of a newborn, Christopher Patterson, told us what prompted him to send a special thank-you to his mother. Here is what he said:

When my wife delivered our first child, a ten-plus pounds boy, I watched his arrival with awe and enormous admiration for my wife's stamina. Days later, it dawned on me what my own mother must have gone through when she delivered my twin brother and me within minutes of each other. Together we had weighed nearly fifteen pounds! I felt as though I should send her a sympathy card. Instead, I sent her this thank-you note:

October 12, 1998
Dear Mom,
I am sitting here just watching Josh (your new grandson)
sleep. [1] He looks so peaceful, I wonder if he's having his
first dreams. Realizing what Daniela went through to
bring Josh into this world, I thought about what it must
have been like when you gave birth to two large redheaded
twins and almost died in the process. [4] And suddenly I
understood from where comes the love of a mother for
her child. [3]

So, this is my frail attempt to say thank you for something so very long past [5], and so very much appreciated
here and now.

I love you [2],
Chris

❧ A Hero Called "Dad"

The wonderful thing about the five basic elements that make a message
clear and dear to others is that they are so easy to use, that anyone—even
young, inexperienced writers—can apply them with great success. To make
this point, take a look at the message below.

In celebration of his dad's fiftieth birthday, a nineteen-year-old was moved
to write this letter. We gave this young man a list of the five basic elements,
and he used our list as a guide when he sat down to write to his dad. We think
this message about a young man's tender feelings for his father is a great example of the genuine and connecting ways you can create deeply touching
messages. Here is the birthday message he wrote:

January 1999
Dear Dad,
Happy fiftieth birthday! [1] I am sitting here at your desk
wondering how to tell you what you mean to me. Well,
here goes. Dad, I will always be glad we had our nightly
talks where we sat and solved the world's problems or
tried to answer strange questions that have no explanation. [4] Like why so many of the women who work at
beauty salons have such ugly hairdos. You even answer
my tough questions about friendship, love, girls and
sports. [3] Also, I will always be glad that we watch TV together. We are the best team of relaxers I know. I love
making fun of soap operas with you.

Dad, you really are my hero. I try to be just like you,
trying to argue and *sometimes* prove things. Even in sports,

I am that little scrapper that you were, too. You *are* my hero, and I admire you, love you and one day want to have a family like you and be as good of a Dad. [2] You always make time to either throw a ball with me or sing or just rap. I want you also to know that it meant a lot to me that you played softball with me last season even though it hurt your knee. If everyone was as honest and caring as you are, the world would be a better and different place. I love the way you laugh when I tell a joke and put your hand on my shoulder and mess up my hair when you walk by me. Also the way you know what the right thing is but you let me experience it in my own way. I remember how you used to let me shift the gear stick in our old car when we were driving along and how when you teach me things you always make it like you're really not teaching. I like that you used to tell me about some of the problems in your office and ask my opinion, and then, if what I said didn't make a lot of sense, you'd sort of nod your head and listen anyway. Whenever you need a favor from me, you turn and ask me not only as your son but also as a friend, and that is how I answer, as a son and a friend. Dad, I know you made your father the best man at your wedding, and I want to do the same thing because my father really is the best man. Mom even says I talk and act like you so much, and it's because you really are what I want to be when I grow up. You are also a model to me of how to help others; you have always shown me how to help, and you are the main reason I want to help people. You have worked hard for everything you have, and you deserve it all and more.

When you look at me, I am happy because I see pride in your eyes. I am proud of you, too. I may grow up and be more independent, but no matter what, I will always have time for a nightly talk or a late night TV session with you. Girlfriends and other people will always come and go, but a best friend, a best man and a father all in one can never leave my heart. [5] I love you.

❧ *Double-Dating*

A year after the death of his mother, our friend "Bill" told us how concerned he was about his father. "Dad looks so down and seems so lonely," he said. "I just wanted to tell him it would be OK with me if he started dating. So I used the elements in your book and tried to write a letter telling him that. But

I got all hung up about butting into his personal business."

Because Bill felt uneasy about his ability to write this without seeming to be lecturing his father or, worse, acting as if he was a know-it-all, we suggested that he begin by putting his purpose on paper.

<u>The gift I want to give you in this message:</u>
<u>My support if you want to go out and find love again</u>
<u>because I love you very much and want you to be happy</u>
<u>in any way you choose to be.</u>

Once he'd put his purpose on paper, Bill's worries about discussing something that was none of his business seemed to dissolve. With a sense of relief, he moved ahead and created the message below.

Notice how this letter blends humor and warmth with genuine concern and practical advice. We think it is a good example of the creative ways that people have put messages together using all the basic elements:

> December 1, 1997
> Dear Dad,
> How weird is this? We're both grown men and now we're both eligible bachelors—in fact, we could actually double-date! It's been over a year since Mom died. [1] I know that you miss her a lot but I hate seeing so much loneliness in your eyes. You have always been the guy I can turn to and trust [3], so I want to encourage you to get back out there and start dating. [5]
> I know it's been over forty years since you asked a woman out, and, yes Dad, things have changed since then. You know all that advice you gave me when I first started dating? [4] It's pretty much obsolete now. So, I'd like to re-turn the favor of giving you advice about what you called "how to treat a lady." I call it "how to interact with women."
> Here's what I learned the hard way. (Remember how you'd see me slumped over the phone as one woman after another turned me down? [4] Well, I finally figured a few things out.)
> 1. The words *lady* and *girl* are out. The word *woman* is in now.
> 2. It's still OK to hold the door open and help a woman in and out of the car—if she doesn't like that, she'll let you know.
> 3. Don't be surprised (or offended) if your date offers to pay her own way.

4. Condoms still fit in a man's wallet—but these days plenty of women keep condoms in their wallets, too.

5. Not all condoms are equal—and preventing pregnancy is not their most important function. Some do a better job of protecting against sexually transmitted diseases than others do, so it's a good idea to find a pharmacist and ask questions!

6. When you get home from a date, if you feel as though you had a nice time, she probably did, too (that's one I learned from you and it's still true).

7. Women don't mind calling a man up and asking him out, and no, that doesn't mean she's what you call "fast"; it just means she likes you.

The good news is you're about to be the Mr. Popularity of your age group. The other good news is that to me, you're still just my pop and I know that if you think this is none of my business you'll let me know. And, if you do, I'll let it go at that. I love you and want to see that old glint back in your eyes again soon. [2]

Bill

➤ *Her Grandmother's Way With Words*

There are times, when we stop to think about some of the older people we know and care about, that we can't help but realize age takes its toll and that our elderly loved ones will not be around forever. It seems as if we can almost hear the clock ticking. And that's when our wish to reach out and connect with older people often pushes us to take action.

This note from a middle-aged woman to her ninety-something grandmother falls into the category of messages written with the sense that time may be running out. The sender told us that her grandmother had been the one source of safety she'd had as a child and she wanted to make sure she had thanked her while there was still time. But, as the woman who wrote this tried to put her thoughts and feelings on paper, she was so overcome with fear that her grandmother might not be around very much longer that she found it almost impossible to keep writing.

To help her, we gave her a copy of the letter from "Amy" that you read in chapter three, and we talked with her about dumping her fears in the right-hand margin as she went along.

The finished letter this woman sent to her grandmother did not include the words she dumped in the margin, but we have left them in the example below so that you can see, once again, how helpful writing in the margins can be when your emotions are running high. Here is the woman's letter and her margin notes:

What She Wrote:

What She Was Thinking:

December 1998

Dear Gram,

One of my New Year's resolutions is to tell the people who helped me in the past that I'm glad they were there for me. And you are the very first person I thought of. [1] I bet you don't have any idea how much you helped me when I was a little girl. So now I'm going to tell you. [5]

I don't want this to sound like I think she's dying

And I don't ever want her to die. I am so afraid.

I knew if I ever needed money, I could turn to you. Even though I never did that, just knowing you were there kept me from feeling desperately alone. You taught me to tell the truth, and then you didn't fall apart or get angry when I told you some truths you didn't like. [4]

She helped me in so many quiet ways.

I remember the day she asked me if I was a virgin, good Lord!

One day, I asked you how on earth people could stay married to each other for years and years without feeling bored or trapped. You pointed to the couple sitting outside your kitchen window and said, "Look at them." I saw Uncle S. and Aunt I.—who'd been married for more than forty-three years then—laughing together. Then you said a good marriage requires a good sense of humor and the ability to let small things roll off your back like "water off a duck." I learned something important from you that day. [3] You also have a wonderful way with words and you gave me a bunch of sayings that have guided me through my life like— "never borrow trouble," "she's more to be pitied than censured," "it's better to give someone money than to make them a loan" and "you've got to have faith."

Gram, you know what my favorite

If not for Gram, I might never have seen what a happily married couple looks like.

Those old sayings of hers are like rules for happy living.

expression of yours is? It's when you look at me and you sing, "There she is, the girl who made me a grandma," to the tune of "Here She Comes, Miss America." Whenever I see you, I hear a song in my head too, "There she is, my Grandmama, the lady who gave me a place to belong." I love you! [2]

I can still hear her singing that to me. Please let her live. I don't ever want her to be gone!

I love her more than I ever said to her before.

❧ *A Teacher's Lasting Lesson*

This is another letter of appreciation for a special older person. Here, a man who had fond recollections of a former teacher took the time to thank her. Even a brief letter that applies the basic elements can become a heartwarming and treasured message:

> October 18, 1996
> Dear Mrs. P.,
> It's been thirty-five years since I was a student in your high school English class, and by now, you probably don't even remember me. But I have never forgotten you, and you're on my mind at the moment because I just finished reading a magazine article about people and their favorite teachers. [1]
>
> You were my favorite teacher in high school [2], and you taught me something I remember every day. [3] I wanted to thank you for teaching me humility.
>
> How did you do that? Well, when you wrote this in my high school yearbook [4]:
>
>> If ever I should be so fortunate as to have a son, I would wish for him many of the qualities I see in you. However, all heroes have a "tragic flaw" as you know—see that yours is not an excess of pride. No quality sits quite as well with greatness as true humility.
>
> I didn't know what you meant and I had to look *humility* up in the dictionary. That's how I learned it!
>
> And it's probably one of the best things anyone ever taught me. So many, many thanks. [5]
> Best regards,
> H.

7

Romantically Speaking

$\mathscr{F}$rom three simple words to lengthy poetic verses, from candy kisses to hearts around lovers' names on the trunk of a tree, the ways you can express your love are endless. Romantic messages don't have to be flowery, poetic or even very long. And you don't have to sound like Romeo or Juliet to connect your message to someone else's heart.

Many people find that concrete expressions of their romantic feelings fall by the wayside when the honeymoon is over, after the kids come along or just because they get so caught up in the events of their everyday lives.

But it really doesn't have to be that way. The people whose stories and letters you are about to read make it pretty clear that creating tangible messages filled with love is simple and enjoyable.

❥ He's No Shakespeare But...

Sitting at the coffee shop one afternoon as we worked on this book, "Glen," a man whom we had met only once before, came rushing up to our table. Glen's wife is one of the people who helped us proofread an early draft of our book. Since she was out of town at the time, we were surprised to find out that Glen had driven all the way over to the coffee shop hoping to talk with us. Grinning and waving a piece of paper excitedly, he said this:

Guess what I just did? I wrote a love letter to my wife! I mean it's Valentine's Day and all and so I knew I should do something since she's away taking care of her father, but I figured I'd just send flowers like I usually do. Only I had a few spare moments this morning, so I leafed through that manuscript of yours that Gloria's been helping you with and all of a sudden I thought to myself, I bet I could write her a love letter. I never have you know. Not that she hasn't asked me to write to her. Gloria's probably asked me to write her something romantic a hundred times since the day we got married. But it's not my style. I'm not good at that sort of thing.

The sad truth is that I feel like I've probably let her down. She's stopped saying that, but I can tell that she's pretty disappointed that I never wrote her a love letter.

So, after I saw in your book where you say that all you have to do is follow five steps—well, I sat down and bingo, out came this letter.

Take a look. I know it's too late to put it in the mail now, but her father has a fax machine at home so I am going to fax it to her as soon as you guys read it. I think I want you to check it against all the elements to make sure I got this thing right. OK?

Here is Glen's love letter to Gloria. We think he got everything right, but more to the point, so does Gloria:

2/14/00

Dearest,

Today is Valentine's Day, and on this special day you're on my mind and inside my heart more than ever. [1] We both know I'm no Shakespeare, but I want you to know that I love you and miss being able to tell you that with a hug in person today. [2] You are out of town taking care of your dad, and I'm sitting on the back porch thinking about the many things that make you so special and unique: your ability to make and keep lifelong friends; your loyalty and devotion to friends and family; your way of teaching our daughter the values of family, friends and helping people in times of need or when they just need a little help; your focus and dedication to getting a job done; your willingness to be a work in progress.

And dear, here are some very special things that you may not know: I love the way you laugh out loud when you're talking on the phone. It makes me feel that all is right with the world. [3] I have learned from you the importance of calling my own family and friends just to keep in touch and not because there is an emergency. It makes me chuckle when I think that you and I like J. Roget (our favorite, high-class special event cocktail) better than Dom Perignon. I admire your personal relationship with God and your bravery and willingness to not mince words with

God or your church when you are displeased with the way the world is running. No one will ever accuse you of not having a mind of your own.

I don't know if I've ever told you how very much I love the way we got married. [4] Not only did we get married for the right reasons, but for me, it was the most intimate and wonderful ceremony that I could have imagined. And what touches me most is that through thick or thin (and Lord knows we have been through the thin), you are there for me. Even though I don't tell you that often enough, I know it in my heart.

What I hope you will get from my message is that even though I don't tell you nearly enough, you are always in my heart. [5]

I love you.

✦ *Love and a Surprising Twist*

Inside an anniversary card, a friend of ours wrote a note to thank her husband for his love, friendship and support. Because she is a particularly reluctant writer, she added in each of the five basic elements, one at a time, in the same order in which we first presented them to you in chapter two. Our friend worried that by writing her feelings down using our formula (her words for the basic elements) her message would turn out to be boring or trite. But that is not what happened.

Instead, her words took a surprising twist. She found herself revealing deep feelings that she'd been afraid to bring up with her husband in person. We wanted you to see her enormous and generous gift of the heart because it is a wonderful example of what can happen even if you add the basic elements into your messages in a set fashion. This is what our friend told us:

> *I'd wanted to say these things to Allen before, but I never did because I hated thinking about a time when only one of us would be around. Only, when I was thinking about how our lives have been filled with so much joy, I couldn't help noticing that awful sense of worry I get when I admit that someday one of us will be left behind. I guess an anniversary card isn't the usual place to tell someone that you love him so much that even if you aren't around you want him to find another love, but that is what I was thinking and those words just seemed to pop out! I felt like I needed to write this—probably because it was easier for me to write it than it would have been for me to try and say it.*

Here is a small portion of the final draft of her anniversary card message:

May 1998

For my husband on our twenty-fifth—can you believe that
anniversary? [1] So many years together and I still smile
when I tell someone I'm your wife. You are the best and
dearest love of my life. [2] I think my favorite thing about
you is how romantic you are. [3] I still can't believe you got a
marching band to play "Moon River" outside my apartment. [4] Then you had all of them get down on their knees
with you, when you asked me to marry you! How lucky I
am that you make such a big fuss over me.

And now I want to tell you something, but I don't want
either one of us to make a big fuss over it. I just want this to
be one way that I can let you know how much I love you. So
here it is. Someone once told me that people who were happily married prove it by remarrying if their spouse dies... I
think that's true. So Allen, if I go first, I want you to get
married again [5], and if anybody out there hassles you
about this, just show them the next two words—ready?

Back off!

Here's hoping we get at least another twenty-five wonderful years together.

Love,

Guess Who

➤ *Love—Wow!*

Below is a simply worded note written by a young man named Benjamin
Mathes to his first love. We think his letter rings especially true. The young
woman who received it agrees and said she plans to "keep it always." Here is
what Benjamin wrote:

January 16, 1998

My love,

This probably won't be a very long letter because I am in the
middle of studying for my test tomorrow but I keep thinking about you, so I decided to take a break and tell you that I
love you. [1] I don't know how this happens, but anytime
I'm with you, I don't seem to have unhappy thoughts of any
kind, ever. That is one of the most wonderful things about
you and what it is like for me to be with you. You know
those times when you tell me I look unhappy? [4] When I'm
with you, I am *not* unhappy! If my face looks unhappy, all
that means is that things are hectic. And, when you're not

around, and I feel all this pressure, I want you to know that
all I have to do is think of you [5]—your eyes, your smile,
your voice, your laugh, anything about you—and right away
I feel better and happy. [3] I love you so much. [2] I feel one
emotion right now—LOVE. Wow! Thank you. Eternally
yours,
    Benjamin

Inviting someone to remember a moment that the two of you have shared
(element 4, What do I remember and treasure about our times together?)
doesn't have to be a long, drawn-out effort. Using just nine words, "those times
when you tell me I look unhappy," Benjamin drew his girlfriend back into a
shared experience.

✦ A Wigged-Out Woman

Finally, we wanted you to see the next message, which is one of the most
endearing and delightfully romantic messages we came across. Actually it is a
videotape that was made by a woman named "Beth" to cheer her husband up
during a time when he was under a lot of financial pressure.

We hope you will notice it took her only ten sentences to add all five basic
elements to the label she put on her tape. Here is what she wrote on the videotape label:

November 1999
Dear Todd: I made this tape for you because I know how
worried you've been lately about all the hospital bills we
have to pay. [1] I can see how tense you are. But I want to
remind you that I love you very much and that we're in
this thing together, remember? [2] Two years ago when I
married you, it was for better or worse.[4] And even
though things are tough now, we still have each other. As
far as I'm concerned, that's all I need, and as far as I'm
concerned, that is what makes things "better." Simple but
true. So take a deep breath, relax, remember that we both
have good jobs and enjoy this silly show that I made to remind you that we can always laugh together. [5] I love the
sound of your laughter and I miss it. [3] Now, on with the
show!
    Beth

When the tape begins we see Beth trying on different wigs that range from
an extreme Afro look to an exaggerated imitation of a silky, long-haired red-

head with so much hair she was practically buried underneath it all.

Each wig looks more ridiculous than the one before. And, as the video-tape unfolds, we see her rolling her eyes and grinning contagiously.

Beth told us that she wanted her husband to know this:

I love him, we can always laugh together and laughing doesn't cost money. I wasn't certain he'd know what I was trying to do, so, I sang a made-up song that went something like this:

Isn't it funny how I've gone wiggy over you,
   isn't it funny how much we still can do,
don't need no money as long as I have you.

OK, so the lyrics aren't great. But the hug I got, the laughter I heard and the smile I saw on his face was priceless! It's been six years since I made that videotape, and sometimes we still pull it out, watch it and laugh together.

8

Passing Along Your Favorite Memories

$\mathcal{M}$ ost of us have our own personal collections of wonderful little moments that stand out in our minds. When we remember these special moments, we often smile and think about the people that matter most to us.

The messages in this chapter will show you some ways to capture your special memories so solidly that they can be passed along and shared with others.

Each of the next four messages retells and shares a favorite memory. The people who made these messages used different styles (dialogue, questions and answers, and lists) and a variety of forms (a note attached to a recipe, hastily scribbled index cards and a videotape). However, as different as they are from one another, all these messages use the same basic elements and demonstrate that when it comes to capturing your memories, your options are endless!

♦ *By Cook or by Crook*

Whenever you create messages that give others a richer understanding of the value your personal treasures hold, you bring those treasures to life. That's what this message does. Inside a birthday letter for her twenty-one-year-old son, a mother told the tale of a long dead scoundrel relative and shared his recipe for hot buttered rum:

> July 1994
> Dear Josh,
> Happy twenty-first birthday! [1] You've always had a strong

sense of family. You complain if I throw out letters or photos, and that's something I'll always remember with love about you. [3] So this recipe for hot buttered rum is one of your presents. I got it from my grandmother who was a very proper woman who claimed our family came over on the *Mayflower*. She was embarrassed that this recipe came from her bootlegging grandfather who supplied liquor back when it was illegal to do that in this country.

She said that sometime in the 1920s, your Great-Great-Grandpa Daniel had to have his right leg amputated. Some people thought losing a leg was a terrible misfortune, but not Grandpa D.!

The first thing he did when they let him out of the hospital was get himself fitted with a wooden leg. Then, he got his car fitted with a false bottom. For years after that, Grandpa D. drove all the way to Canada every six months or so and filled that car's false bottom up with rum! On his way home, he'd have to go through U.S. Customs inspections where everyone was asked to step out of their cars. Your Grandpa D. would stop, open his car door and point to his wooden leg with a big sigh. Feeling sorry for him, the inspectors just waved him right on through.

Grandpa D. never sold his rum. He stored it in his basement. Then every December he threw a party for the whole town. Maybe you'd like to do something like that too because you include people in your life whether they are rich or poor, and that's another thing I like about you! [4] Top officials and all the ne'er-do-wells were invited and everyone had a wonderful time. The secret to their wonderful time? This recipe! So, every holiday season, why not drink a toast to the feisty old guy who concocted it? [5] Cheers!

I love you [2],
Mom

One thing that struck us when we read this woman's message was how clearly it shows the way that time can affect our reactions to family lore. Years ago, mentioning a bootlegging family member might have triggered embarrassment, shame or denial. Today, the same secret seems almost quirky and endearing.

❖ Her Index of Remembered Moments

Here is another quick and simple way that our friend, "Mary Beth," found to capture her favorite memories. We have included two of her messages here because we wanted you to see that it really is easy and heartwarming to make messages that preserve your favorite memories.

In her kitchen, Mary Beth has a small box filled with 3" x 5" index cards. It looks like something you might use to file away your recipes or to organize your grocery store coupons. But Mary Beth uses it for something entirely different:

Every so often, I sit at my desk, pull out these index cards and jot down my thoughts about the funny or sweet things that my children have done lately. I'm not one for taking lots of pictures and I am not good at keeping a journal, so index cards are my way of recording the little human moments in my children's lives.

To make it easy, I use tabbed dividers to separate each child's section. Then I use more dividers so that I can just drop new cards into the box according to the year I wrote them. My kids don't know I do this—I think it'll be a nice surprise for each of them if I give them their own section of my memory index cards as a gift when they get married.

Here are two examples of what Mary Beth writes on her index cards:

1983—April 3
Christie—Today, you pushed your baby mouth right up to mine and whispered that you love me. [1] I hugged you and then I asked you why you whispered into my mouth (instead of my ear) and you said, "Cause that's where your words come out, Mommy." [4] Christie, I love you! [2]
 I am still laughing at your wonderful, logical, adorable three-year-old way of seeing the world. [3] I hope you will always be willing to tell me just how things seem to you because whenever you do that, I get a chance to see the world differently, too. [5]

1986 – December 23
Cody—A little while ago Daddy came in shaking his head and told us the car battery died. [1] You burst into tears. That sure took us by surprise. You looked so sweet [3] when you told us you felt sad because something died. [4] So, we sat down together—the three of us—and talked about all the cycles of life. After that you went back out to play.

Thinking about that, I am filled with love for you and a little bit of wonder, too. [2] Here's what I wonder: Maybe we also should have talked about the differences between objects, like car batteries, and living things, like people. [5]

❧ *Wisdoms and Wisecracks*

Here is a message that we think captures the character, humor and warmth of someone who is no longer here. We liked everything about this message—from the way it made us laugh out loud to its meaningful contents, and especially the clear and dear way that the man who made it described the memories he has of his father. We'd also like you to notice that the sender was so bent on making his intentions known that he applied element 5 (*What do I want you to get from my message?*) twice in his message, with the words "to make sure that you get to have the kinds of wisdom that my father gave to me" and "I would like each of you to hang onto this list and pass it down to your children."

The man who wrote this message is a relative of JacLynn's. He sent it to us to put in our book because he was proud of the way it turned out. (Yes, he created this message by applying the five elements.) This is what he told us about why he made this message:

My father died six years ago. Some of the images I have of him are already fading away. I wanted to share his words of wisdom with my kids and their kids and so on—right down the line. So, I made a list of the clever, wisecracking words of advice that my dad had peppered me with throughout my life. Then last year, on the anniversary of his death, I gave copies of this list to everyone in the family. Here are some of the things I wrote:

December 27, 1997
Dear Family,
Even though (as of today) he's been gone for six years now, I still miss my dad. That made me think about you and how much each of you means to me. [1] We have been through so many years of blessings and tragedies together [4], and I am always so glad I was born into such a loving family. [3] Then I thought some more about my dad and I wondered how much of him you will be able to remember. I love you all [2] and want to make sure that you get to have the kinds of wisdom that my father gave to me. [5] That's why I am writing this note. Dad was one of the finest people God ever made. I learned a lot from him.
     When I look back on things, it seems to me that he was always teaching me about life. But he did it in an un-

usual way—with dry humor and clever quips that I want to share with you in this note. I would like each of you to hang onto this list and pass it down to your children. That way my father can continue to advise all of us. [5]

> Wisdoms and wisecracks from my dad:
> Investing in the stock market—"Never gamble with scared money."
> Dating—"Son, just remember, every girl you ever date is somebody's daughter."
> Loyalty to a place of business—"Fine, but keep in mind, the company never loves you back."
> Donating to an annual fund—"Pace yourself. The ceiling quickly becomes the floor."
> About marriage—"Once the words are out, you can't put them back."
> More about marriage—"There is and always will be only one acceptable answer to the age-old question, 'Does this dress make me look fat?'"

◆ *Hello, My Name Is Ethel*

Recently someone showed us a videotaped message that had been made by an elderly woman named Ethel over a period of seven years. Ethel had died a few years before we saw the two-hour videotape she'd left behind. Obviously, we cannot present her lengthy message here. What we can do, however, is use some of Ethel's own words to explain what prompted her to leave this delightful message behind for someone she will never meet. We hope her words will inspire you to reach out to future generations in an equally powerful way. Ethel began making this videotape at the age of eighty. Here are her opening words:

> Hello, my name is Ethel. Today is March 23, 1989. Our family has a tradition of naming our children after those who have died ; it's a way of keeping faith with the people who have come before us. I sort of like this tradition. [4] So, since I won't actually meet my namesake, I am making this videotape to tell him or her something about me. [1] My neighbor George is using his camera to help me make this.
>
> I was named for my Great-Grandfather Ethan, and I know almost nothing about him but I've always wondered what kind of person he was. Of course, now there's no one around to answer that question, and back when there were people who could, the ones I asked only had a few sketchy

memories of Ethan.

So, in case you'd like to know about me—the person you were named for—I'm leaving you some information on this tape. [5]

When I look in the mirror these days, I see an old woman but I used to be rather pretty and I had plenty of beaus. Growing up, I was a rather stubborn person I suppose. Too stubborn to get married and settle down is the way my parents saw things. You see, back then married ladies didn't work unless they had to, and when they did, it was doing things like teaching, nursing or sewing. But I wanted to be a reporter. I thought getting married would mean giving up my dreams. So I made my choice and it ended up pretty well, because for almost forty-five years I was the only lady reporter in this town besides the society page editor.

Now, I'm not saying you shouldn't get married. When I was coming up, a woman who wanted to work and be married, too—well, it just wasn't done. But today women can have a husband and children and satisfying work all at the same time. If I was brought up today, I might have made a different life for myself, but overall I'm pleased with how things turned out.

I am leaving this scrapbook to my namesake, who I imagine is someone like me and finds other people fascinating. [3] Inside are many of the articles I've written over the years. These articles are sort of like my children. Most of them are my interviews of the extraordinary people I met—people who changed the world a little bit, like Adlai Stevenson who was vice-president and ran for president of the United States. I worked on his election staff. When he lost the election, I was heartbroken. He was a brilliant man. And there's an interview with Helen Keller, who showed the world that handicaps only are handicaps if you let them be. There's also an article I wrote about a dwarf (I think now we call them "little people") who became a fine actor, and many other stories about people who fascinated me.

Well that's all I want to talk about today. Next time, I will tell you other things, like how it felt to watch my men friends go off to war, how I finally learned to believe in

God and what I think of people who use plastic surgery to look younger than they really are. My goodness, I do have a lot of ground to go over, don't I?

Well, George is tired of holding up that camera for now—but just one more thing: I am sorry that I won't meet you personally, dear namesake, but I want you to know that even so, I bet you are someone I'd like. [2] Good-bye for now.

9

Giving Advice That No One Has Asked For

*T*he urge to give advice is wonderfully human. So is the urge to resist it. When the people you care about are going through tough times or struggling to make important decisions, it's natural to want to offer them some advice that you think could help.

But what if your advice hasn't been asked for? What if the person you are concerned about is dealing with a problem that is private, sensitive or seemingly too embarrassing to discuss? Maybe he's out of work, wondering whether or not to get married or distressed by his own aging process.

And what if the people you'd like to advise are the very people who have guided you since birth—your own parents? This reversal in your roles can trigger discomfort in you and it might unleash anger or resentment in your parents.

Then there's all that stuff that comes up if you're the parent of adult children. Longtime child-rearing habits are hard to change, but if you approach your adult children the same way that you did when they were young, you may make it more difficult for them to be willing to consider your suggestions.

Perhaps the easiest kind of advice giving there is takes place between good friends and people who are about the same age as one another. In those cases, there's often a sense that both of you are on equal footing, which seems to make it easier to deliver advice in gentle, offhanded ways. Something about this lighter approach helps your words penetrate deeply and be taken in more fully.

Still, no matter what the age differences or changing roles between you and the people you'd like to advise, it *is* possible to express yourself so clearly and gently that others will find value in your messages.

Creating tangible messages using the five basic elements is a good place to begin; however, there are two additional elements that can really help.

Two Special Elements for Messages of Advice

There are two elements that when added in any order to your messages of advice make it easier for you to communicate your desire to help the other person. And using these elements leaves the receiver feeling more open to your words.

YOU DECIDE

The "You decide" element simply calls for you to include a direct statement that lets the other person know that your feelings will not be hurt and there won't be any negative consequences from you if she chooses a different course of action.

Using this element can be as simple as the example below:

> Feel free to act on my suggestions or not. Either way I sure
> hope things go well for you.

Applying this element lets the receiver know that you respect her right to take your advice or not. And it helps you offer advice in the form of a suggestion rather than as a command (which can leave a person feeling resentful).

HOW I LEARNED THIS

The "How I learned this" element encourages you to describe what you have learned in the past that led you to believe in your own words of advice. Whenever you share your personal experiences (by telling a story or adding in the details of a relevant event), the receiver can connect more deeply with you and more fully understand your offer of advice.

Here's one way to use this element:

> Sorry you got hit by the downsizing that's going on these
> days. It stinks! I know because over the past thirteen years
> I've been "let go" and "downsized" twice. For what it's
> worth, I found a few things to help me hold it together
> when I looked for another job.

When you add in this element, you give the receiver a fuller picture of the experience you've had with the particular issue or problem that you are advising her about. When you do that, you expand the credibility of your message.

How to Apply These Elements

To show you how these two elements help people get their words of advice across fully and with impact, we are going to look at several versions of a letter written by a man named "Martin." Martin is another one of our coffee shop acquaintances. He created this message of advice for his daughter, "Teresa," who was trying to decide whether or not to marry the young man who'd recently proposed to her.

It took Martin three drafts to make a final version of his message. But when he did, he was so pleased with it (and with the reaction he got) that he allowed us to show you what happened when he put his purpose on paper and then added in the two special elements of advice.

Below is Martin's first draft, in which he applied only the five basic elements because he didn't know about the two special elements: *You decide* and *How I learned this.* Here's what he said when he showed us what he'd written in his first draft:

> *I guess I must have done something wrong because I know better than to send my daughter this letter. It'll get me nowhere and probably just push her farther away from me. I don't know what happened here. I used all the basic elements in your book and my letter has all kinds of nice things in it but it just doesn't go anywhere. Would you look it over and tell me what I can do to write something that will help my daughter more than this?*

Here is Martin's first draft:

> December 1999
> Dear Teresa,
> I know that Tom proposed to you. You haven't said anything to me about that, but I am sitting here thinking about you and this big decision you are going to make. [1]
> So I decided to write you a letter. I hope you know that I love you. [2] There are so many reasons that I feel this way that I am having a hard time picking just one. One of the many reasons I love you comes from watching you with the kids in the rehab ward at the children's hospital where you work. Their eyes light up when they see you. You have

quite a talent with them! [3] I noticed this about you back when you took that volunteer job helping three handicapped kids for a whole summer when you were only fourteen. [4] You were so gentle and kind to them that it made me proud.

What I want you to get from this letter is that I hope you will make the right decision about whether or not to marry Tom. [5] I am a lot older than you and I know more about these things. I really think you better talk to me before you make up your mind. There is so much for you to consider, and I am worried about what you will decide. I guess your Mom and I didn't give you the best example of a good marriage, and that makes me worry even more. If you want to talk about things, you know I'm just a collect call away.

Love,

Dad

As he was talking to us about his concerns for his daughter, Martin expressed his loving intentions quite clearly. But his feelings and his reasons for writing to Teresa didn't come across nearly as well in his letter.

In fact, in his letter, Martin seemed to be beating around the bush and not coming to the point as fully as he did when he talked with us. So, we asked him to take another shot at writing to Teresa and to begin by putting his purpose on paper. Martin agreed to try.

The gift I want to give you in this message:
A way to learn from the mistakes I've made and some
information about the things I now believe are
important to think about if you want to make
a good marriage.

We told Martin that when we created our own letters of advice, we found that it was easier to stay on track if we kept our written purpose near enough to keep looking at it as we moved along.

So, Martin tried that, too. Later on he told us that keeping his eye on his written purpose had helped a lot because it kept reminding him of his intention: "What I wanted was for my letter to be a gift to Teresa, not another apology for being a long-distance father or for screwing up my marriage to her mother. So when I compared my purpose to my first draft, I crossed out a bunch of words."

You can see the words that Martin took out when he realized they didn't conform to his written purpose or as Martin put it, "I got rid of the words that didn't exactly sound like I was giving Teresa a gift":

> December 1999
> Dear Teresa,
> I know that Tom proposed to you. ~~You haven't said anything to me about that, but~~ I am sitting here thinking about you and this big decision you are going to make. [1] So I decided to write you a letter. ~~I hope you know that~~ I love you. [2] ~~There are so many reasons that I feel this way that I am having a hard time picking just one. But~~ One of the many reasons I love you comes from watching you with the kids in the rehab ward at the children's hospital where you work. Their eyes light up when they see you. You have quite a talent with them! [3] I noticed this about you back when you took that volunteer job helping three handicapped kids for a whole summer when you were only fourteen. [4] You were so gentle and kind to them that it made me proud.
>   What I want you to get from this letter is that ~~I hope you will make the right decision about whether or not to marry Tom. I am a lot older than you and I know more about these things. I really think you better talk to me before you make up your mind. There is so much for you to consider, and I am worried about what you will decide. I guess~~ your Mom and I didn't give you the best example of a good marriage, and that makes me worry ~~even more.~~ [5] If you want to talk about things, ~~you know I'm~~ just a ~~collect~~ call ~~away.~~
>   Love,
>   Dad

After that, we described the two special elements that are especially important when you are trying to give advice to others. Here's what happened when Martin included the additional special elements:

> December 1999
> Dear Teresa,
> I heard that Tom proposed to you, and I am sitting here thinking about you and this big decision you are going to make. [1]
>   So I decided to write you a letter. I love you very much. [2] One of the many reasons I feel this way comes from watching you with the kids in the rehab ward at the

children's hospital where you work. Their eyes light up when they see you. You have a real talent with them! [3] I noticed this about you back when you took that volunteer job helping three handicapped kids for a whole summer when you were only fourteen. [4] You were so gentle and kind to them that it made me proud.

I'm still proud of you, Teresa, and I've tried to think if I have some advice to give you that might help you decide whether or not to marry your young man. I know that since things didn't work out between your mom and me, I might seem like an unlikely source of advice on what's important in a marriage. But, actually, I have learned something important along the way and I thought if I wrote it down for you here that it might give you something I wish I had known earlier myself.

So what I want you to get from my letter comes down to this one suggestion: When you think about the man you will marry, think about this—do you love this person so much that you can see yourself with him in ten, fifteen, twenty or even thirty years down the road? [5] Please try to be as honest with yourself as you can, because when a marriage ends, you lose a whole lot more than just the love of your spouse. You lose the chance to tuck your little boy or girl into bed each and every night (in the best-case divorce, children spend time—important special time—away from you when they visit their other parent). You miss out on some of your children's special firsts (first day of school, first date, first baby-sitting job, first college acceptance, etc.). Teresa, I have watched you work with children, I know how dearly you love those little ones, and that's why I hope you will think about all this with an eye toward your own future children. Your mom and I learned this the hard way. [How I learned this] I hope our mistakes can help you make better choices than we did. But most of all, I want you to know that whatever you decide to do, you can count on me to be happy for you. [You decide]

If you want to talk about any of this, just give me a call. If you don't want to discuss it, that's OK, too. I always love talking with you no matter what the topic is.

I love you,
Dad

Two days after Martin mailed his completed message to Teresa, he got a phone call from her:

> *At first all I could hear was her sobbing. I thought,* Oh Lord, I've messed everything up. She's probably broken it off with Tom because my advice frightened her to death! *But that wasn't what happened. Teresa said she was only crying because my letter was so touching, and then she put Tom on the phone and he asked me for my permission to marry my daughter. How about that?*

❧ Out of Work Is a Full-Time Job

Most of the time, advice flows between people who know each other fairly well or at least have a long shared history. However, in this case you will see a letter that was sent from a fifty-year-old man to someone he knew only in passing.

We wanted you to see this letter because it makes the point that an effective message of advice can be a gift to someone else whether you have known him for a long time or not. We also think this particular letter is a good example of the impact that a message of advice takes on when you include information about your past feelings and experiences (*How I learned this*). Plus, we wanted you to notice the gentle way in which this sender applied the *You decide* element with the words "If you want to talk, give me a call. If you'd rather not, I'll understand."

The man who received this letter said that besides helping him get through a difficult time, it initiated a strong bond of friendship between the two men. Here is the letter:

> March 1998
> Dear Glen,
> I enjoyed meeting you and your wife at church last week.
> It was nice to see that our kids hit it off right away, too. [4]
> So when I heard that you're out of work and going through
> a rough time, I thought I'd drop you this note. [1]
>
> Sorry you got hit by the downsizing that's going on
> these days. It stinks! I know because over the past thirteen
> years I've been "let go" and "downsized" twice. For what
> it's worth, I found a few things to help me hold it together
> when I looked for another job. [How I learned this] Maybe
> they'll help you, too. I'm listing them here because even
> though we don't know each other very well, you strike me
> as a determined person. [2]
>
> As a matter of fact, you remind me of some of my
> other friends. [3]
>
> If you want to talk, give me a call. If you'd rather not,

I'll understand and cheer you on from the sidelines. [You decide] These are some things that helped me:

1. I turned getting work into a full-time job (Mon.–Fri., 9 A.M.–5 P.M.).
2. I made sure I had at least one appointment every weekday even if it was just to follow up on a phone call or a meeting with someone in an area that was unlikely to pan out.
3. I put every contact I made on a separate index card (included the secretary's name, date of contact, etc.), then I put a note in my calendar book to follow up with a phone call in ten days.
4. I told everyone (even strangers at the barbershop) that I was looking for work. This was the hardest one for me because I'm a fairly private person, but I made myself do this. Turns out the guy waiting for his turn in the barber chair heard me and said I should see his cousin at an insurance company because they were looking for help. So I did and they hired me about three weeks later.
5. I got an answering machine that let people leave work-related messages in a separate "mailbox." That helped me sound more businesslike, and it kept the kids from hearing more details than I wanted them to.

Glen, good luck with your search! Hang in there. Hope you know that this sort of thing happens to the best of us, and if you want to call me for lunch, I'd be happy to hear how you're doing. [5]

Regards,
Jerry

❧ In-Laws and Outlaws

We want you to see this next letter because it shows that even when your words of advice are lighthearted offerings, using the two special elements can add depth and value.

This message applies the *How I learned this* special element with the words "maybe it will save you from some of the mistakes and bloopers I stepped in." And the sender's words "Feel free to read it or not" are an effective way to apply the *You decide* element. Read it for yourself:

January 3, 1997
Dear Kim,
Congratulations on your daughter's upcoming wedding.[1]

Ready or not, you're about to be a mother-in-law! We've been friends since we were pregnant with our daughters. I still remember that luckily for me you lived close by and you were always willing to watch the kids when Carl needed my help at the store. [4] You are a great friend. [3] I love you for that. [2]

So friend, here's a book that gave me a crash course on some of the dos and don'ts of mother-in-law-hood.

Feel free to read it or not. [You decide] If you do read it, maybe it will save you from some of the mistakes and bloopers I stepped in [5], like the time I suggested that my daughter might want to exchange the gift my son-in-law gave her for something a little more flattering. [How I learned this] Yeesh!

Welcome to the wacky world of life as an in-law.

Love,

Cindy

➤ *About Those "What If's"*

A mother of three told us that she used to worry so much about what might happen to her children if she died that she was unable to go out and enjoy herself. When her sister gave her some advice that helped her conquer her fears, this woman restated her sister's advice—almost word for word—in a letter for her children. What we hope you will get from reading this message is just what we got: an appreciation for the value of putting on paper the sound advice that others have given us so we can pass it along to people who might also find it helpful.

We also liked the way this woman presented her message by replaying the dialogue between her sister and herself. Flavoring messages with dialogue seems to add a special aliveness to the words. Here is how this woman described what led her to write to her children:

A long time ago, my sister gave me some advice that helped me get over my fears and get on with my life. After that I wrote a letter about what she said to me, and in that letter, I described how her words helped me.

Someday, when my children have kids, I'll give them this letter because it's got some good advice that when they become parents might help them, too.

Here's the mother's message:

November 1989

Dear Cathy, Glen and Corey,

This morning I was watching the three of you play together. Each of you took turns describing what you would do when you grew up. [4] It was such a sweet conversation that I wish I had tape-recorded your words. I love all of you dearly. [2] I am always surprised at how well you get along and how much you look out for each other. [3] That is one of my favorite things about all of you. Since Dad just took you out for ice cream, I decided to use my quiet time to write you this letter. [1] Then I will put it away for you to read when you really are all grown up.

I wanted to tell you that I used to worry about what would happen to you if I died, so much so that I started writing letters about all the things I'd want you to know—you know, just in case. Then I put my letters away someplace safe so, God forbid something should happen, at least you'd know what I want you to do. [5]

Maybe that sounds strange, but writing those letters gave me a chance to square things away and relax. I still do that. Then, I get on with my life!

I started writing letters like that a long time ago when I was supposed to head off on a romantic six-day vacation with your dad (our first in two years). [How I learned this] The thing is, I was afraid to go away. I knew you would be fine with your grandparents for the week. But I still didn't want to leave you. My sister could tell that something was wrong. When she asked me about it, I told her that I was afraid.

"Afraid of what?" she asked me.

"Of all the 'what if's,' " I answered. "What if the plane crashes? What if we're hijacked? What if the guy seated behind me turns out to be a terrorist for crying out loud? What if I die? What if my kids have to grow up without me?"

"Oh, *those* 'what-if's,'" my sister said. "They're easy to fix. Just sit down and think of every terrible thing that could possibly happen. Then, write letters to everybody about everything you're worried about. I mean, they're your kids, right? So, in your letters tell the people you've picked to raise the kids if you're not around what you want them to do. Like what type of school you want your kids to go to, how old you want them to be before they start dating, what their curfew should be, whether you think they should have to help pay for their first car—all that stuff. Write out your worries. Leave your marching orders, and then go out there and live!"

Anyway, I did write that stuff down. Then your dad and I went on our vacation. We had a blast! I smile now when I reread some of those old letters (even the parts where the ink is blurred because I cried feeling all my love for you while I wrote). So, if you ever feel the same kind of worries that I felt, you might want to write letters, too. [5 and You decide]

Love,

Mom

➤ *Beyond Birth Control*

Although we have noticed that many people put the *You decide* element near the beginning of their messages (probably because this element can help relax feelings of wariness in the receivers), in this case that particular element shows up at the end of the message.

The words "I've learned to trust your ability to gather the facts and make wise choices" at the bottom of this note seem to suggest that the sender and the receiver have so much respect for one another that it (almost) goes without saying. See if you agree:

April 28, 1996

Dear Katie,

I have been thinking about our last conversation [1] and about how impressed I was with your clearheaded thoughts about when to have sex and with whom. [4] But I'm writing this because I thought of something I didn't say then.

You told me that you and your boyfriend are virgins, that you know how to protect against pregnancy and that you don't have to worry about sexually transmitted diseases. Still, if you do have sex, I hope you'll do more to protect yourself than just taking the birth control pill. [5]

Here's why [How I learned this]: A friend of mine's daughter may never be able to have children because she and her boyfriend only used the pill. Apparently, they broke up briefly, and during that time, the boy had unprotected sex. Sort of a one-night stand I think. Then when he and his girlfriend got back together, he was too uncomfortable to tell her about his fling.

Anyway, since then, my friend's daughter has had what they thought was pelvic inflammatory disease but it turns out that what she has is more serious than that—she has a sexually transmitted infection that caused such serious scarring she probably won't be able to have children.

I'm not saying that would happen to you but it could, and I love you, so of course I worry. [2] I thought if I told you this that maybe you'd keep it in mind, and when you decide to be intimate with someone [You decide] I hope you'll use condoms along with birth control protection. That way, I'll be able to baby-sit for your children someday. What a nice thought! I'm glad you care about my opinion. I've learned to trust your ability to gather the facts and make wise choices. [3 and You decide]

Love,

Katherine

❧ *By the Book*

Here is another interesting and effective way to deliver advice in a message. This letter is from an older woman, "Aunt Linda," to her young nephew. Right from the start, Aunt Linda did a wonderful job of identifying common ground between herself and the receiver with the comment, "I noticed how much time you spend reading. So do I!" Whenever you use phrases like this, you make it more likely that the people who receive your messages will be open to finding value in your words.

Later in her message, Aunt Linda applies the *You decide* element gently with her words "I've gotten a lot of enjoyment, knowledge and comfort from these books and hope that you'll feel the same way." We believe that using open-ended approaches like this when you are advising others lets them know that you respect their right to follow up or not on your suggestions.

Finally, we especially liked Aunt Linda's descriptions about what she learned from each book on her list. We think those sentences add enormous clarity, impact and value to her message. And her descriptions of what she gained from each book seem to apply the *How I learned this* special element without detailing information that might be too heavy-handed or overwhelming for her young nephew. Here's the letter:

March 28, 1999

Dear Sam,

Last time I visited I noticed how much time you spend reading. [4] So do I! I thought you might like to see a list of some of my favorite books. [1] I've gotten a lot of enjoyment, knowledge and comfort from these books and hope that you'll feel the same way. [You decide] Although I don't see you often, I always enjoy your quick smile. You make me feel welcome [3], so this is my way of saying thanks. I hope you'll have many years to read, learn from and savor these books [5]:

Stranger in a Strange Land, by Robert Heinlein (Amereon, Ltd.), taught me a concept called "Grock," which means to appreciate, respect, connect with and learn from people even when they seem to have strange customs or beliefs.

October Sky, by Homer H. Hickam (Delacorte Press), gave me a way to feel better about my father who hardly ever showed affection.

Don't Sweat the Small Stuff...and It's All Small Stuff: Simple Ways to Keep the Little Things From Taking Over Your Life, by Richard Carlson (Hyperion), helped me stop worrying about all the unimportant hassles in life.

Power: How to Get It, How to Use It, by Michael Korda (Warner Books), helped me get my boss and co-workers to pay more attention to my ideas.

Snow in August, by Pete Hamill (Little, Brown and Company), showed me how people who are so very different from one another can still help each other.

Do What You Love, the Money Will Follow: Discover Your Right Livelihood, by Marsha Sinetar (Dell Publishing), gave me the courage to leave a high-paying job I didn't like and start a new career I love.

Men Are From Mars, Women Are From Venus, by John Gray (HarperCollins), clued me into how and why men see things differently than women.

When Bad Things Happen to Good People, by Harold S. Kushner (Schocken Books), comforted me and convinced me that God was not punishing me every time bad things happened.

Talk Before Sleep, by Elizabeth Berg (Random House), showed me it's OK to miss people who aren't here anymore and reminded me to make my time with people who are count as much as I can.

Sam, if you let me know what you think of these books, I'll swap reactions with you. I'm pretty curious about books, so if you want to make some suggestions about others that you think I might like to read, please do. And if you do, I promise to read them and tell you how they affected me. Take good care of yourself because you sure are a wonderful young man, and with all the reading you do, I bet you're going to be one of the smartest and most amazing people around in the years to come. [2]

Love,
Aunt Linda

◆ Empty Nesting

The realization that the children are leaving but the spouse is not can require couples to redefine their relationships. Here is a message about the challenges that empty nesting brings to a marriage. The woman who wrote this came to a workshop we conducted in the spring of 1999. After she developed her message, she decided to put it away for her children to read many years from now.

In addition to applying the basic elements of a message and the two new elements we have presented in this chapter, we think the sender did a really great job of writing this letter in her own true voice:

> June 1999
> Dear Joey and Megan,
> The oddest things are going on all around me. People who have been married for more than twenty or thirty years are suddenly getting divorced. That got me thinking, and I wanted to write this letter to you even though I don't plan to give it to you until you have grown children of your own. [1] You are both heading off into life on your own, and believe it or not, as much as I love your father, the idea of living the rest of my life in a house with just him was giving me the heebie-jeebies.
>
> It's not that I want to keep you here with us. I don't. You've both grown up so well. [3] But I've been thinking about what it will be like to live the rest of my life with just your dad. For the last twenty years or so, it seems we've been arguing about how to raise you or whether or not to spend money on this thing instead of that.
>
> I guess it is probably normal to wonder what life is going to be like when your children (the glue that holds couples together for years) fly from the nest.
>
> In case you ever feel that way, too, I thought maybe it would help you to know that these feelings are normal and that there are some things you can do to rekindle your relationship before you get too far apart. [5]
>
> One thing we did was go to a marriage counselor about a year ago to start getting ready to be empty nesters. The therapist we met with helped us remember why we got married in the first place, and that made us both smile.
>
> Another thing that helped us was a book called *The Pull of the Moon*, by a woman author named Elizabeth Berg. I read the book first and couldn't believe there was someone

else who understood what it's like to be married for so many years and then—bam—you wonder about who you are and what you really want for the rest of your life.

Your dad read the book, too, and said it made him really understand what it had been like for me to be his wife and your mother for so many years. It felt so good to hear those words from him. We are lucky that we noticed our marriage was feeling shaky and that we didn't just keep our thoughts to ourselves. [How I learned this] It seems to me that the couples who didn't talk with one another before the empty nest time hit them are the ones who haven't made it.

Anyway, now I am actually looking forward to having your dad all to myself. I wanted you to know this because I remember you both telling me that you think your dad and I have the perfect marriage. [4] You may not have noticed that we work pretty hard to keep our love and time together full of joy. I don't know if you'll ever need or want these suggestions [You decide], but if you do, I hope they help you as much as they have us.

I love you [2],

Mom

✦ *To Make Her Life Easier*

As you age, you can arrive at a time when you want (or need) to advise your own parents. That's when putting your thoughts on paper—especially if you're addressing your age-related concerns about them—gives you a way to pick your words carefully and gives your parents time to reflect in private before responding.

The middle-aged woman who sent this letter to her elderly mother found that Writing in the margins was a technique that helped her to finally tell her mother something that she felt strongly about but had dreaded bringing up. Here is how the woman described what it was like for her to broach this difficult topic with her mother:

> *You have no idea how hard it was for me to suggest to my mother that she think about moving into a high-rise community for senior citizens. She is a very proud woman. I was afraid that even mentioning the idea might offend her.*
>
> *I guess the hardest part of dealing with this from my end of things was the guilt I felt about wishing Mom would move someplace where there would be other people besides just me to entertain or help take care of her. I felt ashamed of wishing I could have more time for my own life.*

I could not have dealt with this in a conversation. At first, I wasn't sure I could even do it in a message. I went through three drafts before I came up with a letter that I was willing to send. Using all the basic and special elements in my message and writing in the margins helped me organize my thoughts. I think that is probably what made it easier for my mother to consider making some changes.

Here is this woman's message, and although it was sent to the receiver without the margin notes, we left them in for you to see exactly how writing in the margins helped the sender in this instance:

What She Wrote:	**What She Was Thinking:**
April 1999	
Dear Mom,	
I hope writing this will give me the courage to tell you the truth and offer some advice you'd probably rather not hear. Most of all though, I hope you'll understand how deeply concerned I am and how very much you mean to me. [2]	*This is my third draft. I'm afraid of hurting her or letting her down.*
I just came back from visiting my friend Sarah's mother (remember her from my old sorority days—her name is Ella?). She seemed so happy that I couldn't help wishing you lived there, too. [1]	*My mother looks so much older than Sarah's mom.* *Guilt. I feel guilt! I am being so careful with my words.*
Sarah's mother moved into a senior residence fifteen months ago and told me her life is more enjoyable than it's been in years. [How I learned this] She doesn't have a lawn to worry about. She doesn't have to drive a car because there's a twenty-four-hour van service to take her anywhere in town for free (it's part of her monthly rent payment). She doesn't have to cook unless she wants to because there's a beautiful dining hall, lounge and snack bar in her building. Even bad weather is no problem because a bank, hair salon and library are in the building.	*Am I trying to manipulate her? That's awful but I'm also praying this will work.*

I feel guilty telling you that I wish you lived in a high-rise for senior citizens like Sarah's mom does. But taking you to see your doctors, grocery shopping and on other errands is becoming too much for me. I keep thinking about all the wonderful things you've done for me, and I'm worried you'll think I'm selfish because I just can't keep this up anymore.

As much as she's done for me, I'm ashamed to feel burdened by her, but I do.

Mom, I am so proud of how you've adapted to life without Dad. [3] But I'm not surprised. You've always found creative ways to solve problems. Remember when you took in a boarder to earn money so you could send me to music camp? [4] You told me you were doing that just to have someone around who was tall enough to change the front porch lightbulb. I am so grateful to you, Mom, and I love you so much that I want your life to be easier than it is now.

I know you've always been against the idea of living in an apartment home, but I am asking you to reconsider. [You decide] Mom, you taught me to tell you the truth, and much as I want to be there for you, I can't give you the kind of companionship that Sarah's mother has found with people her own age in her new apartment building. Nor can I give you the kind of peace of mind she says she feels knowing there are nurses on duty if she needs them.

Mom, please keep an open mind. (Sarah's mother said it took her a while to decide to move.)

I love her and worry so much. I'm exhausted.

I hope she's not angry.

Please call me when you've had time to think about this letter. I would like to bring you with me when I go visit Sarah's mother again next week. I hope once you've read this you'll be willing to look at a senior community. I love and respect you and I will do my very best to continue being involved

If she won't move, then we'll have to find another solution.

with and helping you enjoy your life as
much as I possibly can. [5]
    Mom, I love you very much,
    Joanne

➧ *Safety First*

While we were putting this book together, a number of people told us how
uncomfortable they felt talking with older people about the limitations that
aging imposes. Clearly, making messages that deal with the frailties of elderly
people can be difficult for many of us. It may be that we feel some personal
concern about reaching a time when we might not be able to take care of ourselves. Or perhaps we are reluctant to address issues of aging because we are
afraid we might hurt the others' feelings or provoke their anger at us.

So, when someone showed us this message that uses the basic and special
elements to address the issue of aging in a sensitive, loving and honest
manner, we felt it was important to share it with you here.

In the message below, we liked the way the sender worded what he imagined his father might be feeling while reading this letter. It seems to us that
there's something about predicting what we suspect the other person may be
feeling (even when our predictions are inaccurate) that helps our message have
impact.

Although this letter tells someone that it's time to stop driving, the same
approach works well when you want to address other age-related issues, such
as impending retirement, the need for assisted care or a living will, arranging
for power of attorney, etc.:

> August 17, 1999
> Dear Dad,
> I've been thinking about writing this to you for several
> weeks—ever since our last drive together when I noticed
> you had trouble controlling the wheel. [1] When I asked you
> to let me drive, you got very upset. This is a difficult letter
> for me to write to you because I respect you so much and
> I'm worried that reading this will hurt your feelings or
> wound your pride. I also don't want you to be angry with
> me, even though I don't know for sure if that's how you will
> react when you read this. Dad, I love you, and that is why I
> don't feel like I have a choice about writing this. [2] I have
> to risk making you angry at me by telling you that it is time
> for you to stop driving. [5] It is very hard to say that to the
> kind and patient man [3] who taught me to drive in the first
> place! [4] But the facts are that your eyesight and other
> things (which are normal for anyone in his late eighties)

make it too dangerous for you to drive now.

I have been picturing myself getting a letter like this from my son someday, and I think it would make me feel as if my whole world were crashing in. The idea of not being able to take myself anywhere I want to go whenever I want to makes me feel too dependent on others.

Maybe you feel that way, too. Maybe you don't. Maybe you'll be relieved to know that I love you too much to ignore your safety. But there is one thing you taught me that I am sure of: You taught me that it is important to value life—yours and other people's. [How I learned this] I can't make this problem go away. I wish I could. But I do have some ideas that might help you get around whenever you want. Would you please call me after you read this? [You decide] Then I'll come over so we can talk about this face to face. Thanks, Dad.

I love you [2],
Adam

10

Repairing Relationships—
Opening the Door

$\mathcal{I}$n this chapter, you will find messages that bridge the distance, years, hurts, angers, misunderstandings, fears and pride that so often leave people feeling as if they are stuck on opposite sides of a tightly closed door. Unlike expressions of love, which are based on positive feelings, messages to repair relationships are complicated by conflicting negative and positive feelings, such as love and anger. When emotions as powerful as these converge, you can feel pulled in so many different directions at once that you're either unable or afraid to make a move. No matter who or what caused the problem in the first place, unless you want to stay stuck, someone has to open that door!

Deciding to take the first step to reconnect or repair a relationship is a courageous choice filled with hope and possibilities. Getting to a happy ending, however, requires effort and motivation from both people in a relationship. The simple truth is this: You can lead a horse to water, but you can't make it drink, or even share your thirst!

So, how do you take the first step? You might pick up the phone and call the person. Sometimes that works just fine. But when emotions run high or the gap between the two of you seems huge, creating tangible messages can be a more effective way to convey your wish to reconnect.

Below you will see how people used the five basic elements, the two new special elements introduced in this chapter and the techniques of Putting your purpose on paper and Writing in the margins. All together, these are the things that can help you create effective messages even when you are angry, hurt, fearful or disappointed. Regardless of the type of problem or the extent of damage in a relationship, the elements that can help you reach out to repair or reconnect are the same.

Even though most of these stories have happy endings, we have not always shared those with you because our purpose here is simply to show you some effective ways to take the first step toward repairing a relationship.

What Are the Special Elements That Help You Open the Door?

There are two special elements that will help you to initiate a reconnection.

PINPOINT THE PROBLEM WITHOUT BLAMING

Using the "Pinpoint the problem without blaming" element sets the stage, identifies your view of the problem and seems to make it easier for the other person to reply. It also gives the receiver concrete information about how you view the issue(s) between you. When you do this without blaming yourself or others, you make it easier for someone to absorb your words instead of defending against them.

And even if you are apologizing, your message will be more clearly understood if it is free of self-blame and presented as a description of past actions that were less than what you would have liked them to be.

Here are two different ways to use this element. The first statement is good:

> The problem is I feel like we aren't friends anymore.

The second wording is even better:

> The problem is I feel like we aren't friends anymore. You
> have always been such an important part of my life that I
> feel lost without you to turn to.

The difference between the good and even better versions—as always—has to do with the amount of detailed information the sender included.

ASK FOR A SPECIFIC RESPONSE

When you ask for a specific response, you invite the other person to get back to you in a particular way or in a set period of time. Perhaps you want to hear back from him by the end of the week. Or maybe you'd like him to phone you. By asking the other person to respond in a specific way, he can decide whether or not to respond, and your request may inspire him to suggest other solutions. But most importantly, if you ask for a response, you are much more likely to get one, and if you do get a positive reply, then the two of you are reconnected.

Here are two applications of this special element. First, here's the good version:

> Why haven't you been in touch with me? Please tell me.

Here's an even better version:

> Why haven't you been in touch with me? Please tell me either by writing back to me or by calling me.

Again, the difference between a good and even better use of this element is directly linked to the amount of detail you provide and your willingness to express yourself in your true voice.

❧ *One Woman's First Step*

A former patient of Paul's, whom we'll call "Ruth," let us share her experience with you here. She discovered that using the basic elements of a special message along with the two additional elements discussed above made it easier for her to take the first step to reconnect with someone.

Ruth's experience also shows how writing in the margins can help a person focus on and express her positive intentions—even when she has mixed or conflicting feelings about doing so. Paul described Ruth's situation this way:

> *When Ruth first came to see me, she was in her late forties, had been widowed for approximately nine months and felt stuck in her grief and depression. During one of our first sessions together, Ruth told me that when her husband "Mark" died, her lifelong friend "Connie" dropped out of her life, too. Although the two women lived quite a distance from one another, they had maintained a close relationship with telephone calls and visits back and forth. But Ruth hadn't heard from Connie since the day Mark died. When I asked her why she didn't just pick up the phone and tell Connie how hurt she was and how much she missed her, Ruth crossed her arms stiffly and said, "Don't be ridiculous! She should call me!" Through tightened lips, she added, "There are a hundred good reasons why I couldn't possibly call her."*
>
> *"Really?" I said. "A hundred reasons? Let's make a list of your reasons and see what we've got here, OK?"*

Here is Ruth's list:

1. I'm right about what she did; she's the one who's wrong.

2. She ought to make the first move.
3. I'm sick and tired of always being the one who has to reach out to people.
4. I do have *some* pride, you know.
5. What's done is done—no matter what she says, it won't change things.
6. She's probably got new friends now. Obviously she's forgotten all about me.
7. It's too late.
8. I can't forgive her no matter what.
9. I'm scared she wouldn't take my call.

When Ruth looked back over this list, she muttered, "All right, maybe there aren't a hundred reasons but there are enough!"

"Ruth, if you could find a way to get past all your reasons for not calling Connie, would you want to call her?" I asked.

"Yeah," she said, "but so what? It's not possible!"

I suggested Ruth might try an experiment. I asked her if she would be willing to write a letter to Connie knowing that she never had to send it. Hesitantly, Ruth nodded yes. I told her about the five elements of a message and about two more elements that can help a person take the first step toward reconnecting with someone else. Then I showed her some ways that other people had used these elements in letters. I also asked Ruth to keep track of her negative and conflicting feelings by jotting them down in the right-hand margin as she went along. She agreed to try.

The following week, toward the end of our session, Ruth reached into her purse and pulled out a hand-scribbled draft of the letter she'd written to Connie. In a voice shaking with tears, she read what she'd written:

What She Wrote:	**What She Was Really Thinking:**
April 2, 1998 Dear Connie, Lately I have been sad because first Mark died and then you just up and disappeared on me. It's been so long since I've heard from you. [1] I wish you called me or came for a visit. But you haven't, so the problem is I feel like we aren't friends anymore. [Pinpoint the problem without blaming] You have always been an important part of my life and I feel lost without you to turn to. [3] You used to be the	*You probably don't even care how I'm doing.* *I hate telling her I miss her—she probably couldn't care less.*

only one I could count on, and even though you might not care about me anymore, I still miss you. [2]

I remember when you taught me to drive and I smashed your brother's car into the mailbox. And when your mom told you the facts of life and then you told me and we swore we'd never do anything that disgusting. I even think about the day you came over to help me tell my folks that I was going to marry Mark. [4]

Don't these things mean anything to her? I guess not.

Where the hell are you, Connie?

Why haven't you been in touch with me? Please tell me by writing back or calling me. [Ask for response] I wish that you were in my life, but I'm not going to beg you to come back.

This is way too humiliating. I'll be damned if I tell her that!

If I had the guts to mail this, I'd want you to give me some explanation—some way to make sense out of your dropping out of my life when I needed you the most, some way to stop hurting.

Too bad this will never get straightened out.

I'd probably tell you I miss you and love you so you'd remember how things used to be. [5]

Ruth

I miss her.

"Your letter is wonderful! It's direct and very touching," I told Ruth.

"Yeah, for all the good it'll do me. Connie will never see it. She'll never know how I feel and she probably doesn't give a damn!"

I asked Ruth how she could be so certain that Connie didn't "give a damn" about her and added, "It seems to me that you've done a lot of guessing about how she feels. And you're also hiding a lot of your own feelings from her.

"Look at what you put in your margin notes. See how many times you don't come right out and show her your tender or hurt or angry feelings? And how many times you assume you already know what Connie thinks or feels? You've decided that Connie doesn't care about you and that might be true. But what if it's not?" I asked.

"What difference does it make? I'll never know, either way."

"Well," I said, "do you want to know? Because if you do, I know one way you could find out."

"How?"

"You could mail this letter to Connie."

"No way!" she countered.

"OK, that's your choice to make. But tell me what you're afraid might happen if you did mail your letter. What's the worst thing you can imagine?"

"The worst thing that could happen is she'd ignore me and I'd know I was right!" she snapped.

"And, suppose she did ignore you, would that change anything?" I asked.

"No. Well, yes, 'cause then I'd know she doesn't care!" Ruth said.

"And, if Connie didn't ignore you?"

"I'm too afraid to take the chance," she sighed.

"I'll bet," I said. "It takes a lot of courage to risk finding out the truth." Our session ended after that and Ruth left the room slowly, lost in thought.

The following week, breathless and grinning, Ruth said she needed to leave a bit early in order to pick Connie up from the airport. Delighted to see her so happy and alive, I listened as Ruth told me that after our session the week before, she'd gone home and thought about the letter she'd drafted for Connie.

She said, "I looked at everything I'd written inside the letter and in the margins, too. Then I rewrote the letter, but this time I left the list of elements and my margin notes out and mailed it before I could lose my nerve. Three days later, I got this note":

April 13, 1998

Ruthie, thank God you wrote to me. I thought it was you who disappeared on me! When I didn't come to Mark's funeral, you never called me again and I was afraid you were too angry to forgive me.

I couldn't come to Mark's funeral because I had to have some surgery that same day. I didn't tell you that back then because I didn't want to worry you, what with everything else that was going on. Anyway, it turns out that I'm fine. Except for missing you. I am coming to see you Thursday at 6 P.M.

Please meet me at the airport if you can. Otherwise, you'll find me on your front doorstep. I'm not leaving till we get this worked out!

Love,
Connie

❧ *A Mother's Guess*

Here is a note sent by a mother to her grown daughter. The sender uses all the basic and special elements of a message. We especially liked the way she explained her view of the problem without blaming herself or her daughter (*Pinpoint the problem without blaming*). We also liked the manner in which she shared her train of thought. The words "I may be off base about what's going on between us, but this is my best guess" make it possible for the receiver to confirm or modify her mother's guesswork.

Finally, we liked the simple and direct way in which this woman invited her daughter to participate in solving the problem (*Ask for a specific response*) with the words "Next time that happens, would you please tell me to stop?" Here is her complete message:

> March 18, 1987
> Dear K.,
> Lately it seems to me as though everything I say annoys you. [1] The problem is I feel like I am walking on pins and needles whenever you stop by. I hate feeling that way. [Pinpoint the problem without blaming] I've tried to think if I have done something to upset you or hurt your feelings.
>
> I may be off base about what's going on between us, but this is my best guess. I am imagining that you might think that I butt in on your personal life more than I should. So, if this is what has caused the tension between us, I have a suggestion. Next time that happens, would you please tell me to stop? [Ask for a specific response] I promise that I will. I mean it!
>
> I love you [2] and respect your right to decide what you want me to know or not know about your life. I'm so glad you're the kind of person who is willing to keep working on things until they are resolved. Remember when we never could agree on anything when we went shopping together back when you were fifteen or so? It was your idea to stop wasting time by trying to convince each other that one of us was right and the other one was wrong. You said we should just keep going until we found something that both of us liked and that's what we'd buy. Great suggestion! It worked and you taught me a lesson about compromise that I've used many times since then. [4] Sweetheart, you are a great daughter and a treasured friend [3], so let's hang in there and get past this problem, too. [5] OK?
> Love,
> Mom

❧ *His Interfaith Dilemma*

Reaching out to people when you are very angry or terribly hurt takes courage and a great deal of goodwill. And communicating effectively when you are in the midst of an upheaval requires something more: a careful choice of words.

Using the elements can certainly help. But when your feelings are in turmoil, putting your purpose on paper and writing in the margins are especially helpful.

Earlier, you saw the way in which Ruth used writing in the margins to thread her way through misunderstandings, assumptions, sadness and loss. This technique is particularly useful whenever you have negative feelings that are at odds with your positive intention to repair a relationship. This applies equally well to messages that are made in the wake of embarrassing situations, heated arguments or years of silence.

In the next letter, which was created by a young man named "Carl" for his parents, the sender attempts to repair the hurts that his decision to marry outside his faith has caused. Because his feelings were so mixed (love and anger, hurt and longing), he began by putting his purpose on paper.

The gift I want to give you in this message:
Reassurance that Victoria and I love you and we are committed
to finding some way for all of us to get back to being family.

After writing his purpose, Carl communicated his feelings without blaming his parents for theirs and he requested a specific response from them. This letter seems to be a genuine and heartfelt example of the kinds of small steps people can take to address a big issue. Here is the final draft of his letter, which did not include his margin notes:

What He Wrote:

October 22, 1995
Dear Mom and Dad,
I haven't been able to stop thinking about writing to you for weeks now, but I saw so much disappointment in your eyes when I told you that Victoria and I had gotten married that I thought I should wait awhile before contacting you. [1] I want to say how much I love you [2] and that I am intent on finding some way to repair the breach in our relationship.

What He Was Thinking:

I'm sorry they're disappointed but this is my life.

They haven't even given Victoria a chance.

I love them but I'm too angry to feel it.

I know that you were hurt and angry with me when I married Victoria. I have always known you did not want me to marry outside our faith. I really feel badly that this issue has put so much distance between us. [Pinpoint the problem without blaming]

What's done is done. Let's all act like adults and move on.

I want you to know that I did not enter into my marriage lightly and that I thought long and hard about you and your wishes for me when I was trying to decide what to do.

I'm trying to sound mature so that they'll treat me that way.

I doubt this letter will work, but writing it calms me down.

I also thought about how much more difficult things will be for Victoria and me when we start having our own children. We have done a lot of talking with religious leaders of both faiths, and they, too, expect that trying to blend our religions into a solid new family will be difficult. They also told us how important having support from our families will be as we struggle to find common ground and mutual understanding. I remember so many times that were wonderful when I was growing up and how hard you both worked at making our holidays true celebrations. [4] I also remember the emphasis the two of you have always placed on the importance of family. [3] That is why I am hoping that you will be able to rise above the hurt and anger you feel right now so that we can find our way back to being family. [5]

You always said family was everything!

So prove that you mean it and accept my family!

Mom and Dad, I want your approval and blessing and your pleasure in knowing that I come home from work every day to a good and loving wife. I don't know how to reach out to you. But I want to. Victoria does, too. We both need you in our lives. Maybe we could all just meet for coffee and keep it light but still try to find something we have in common. [Ask for a specific response]

Victoria really wants me to keep trying, but if they hurt her again, I'm not so sure that I will.

I'd even be happy if we could just have a conversation about anything. I know this is not a magic bullet—it's just a small step. But it might be a step in the right direction. I will call you on Friday after you have read this letter to see if you can get together with us sometime this weekend or next. [Ask for a specific response] I sure hope so.

Will they agree to go out with us? Hope so.

 Love,
 Carl

❧ Money Matters

Here is a letter that was written by a married woman who hoped to repair a friendship she and her husband had with another couple. Their friendship fell apart because of a misunderstanding about money.

This message identifies the issue between them (*Pinpoint the problem without blaming*) with her words "David is too embarrassed to ask you for the money. And I've been too angry to bring it up before now." The sender invites the receivers to participate in finding a solution (*Ask for a specific response*) by noting, "I'd like to make things right so we can be friends again, but I need your help," and, "How can we settle this? Any ideas?"

Here is what she wrote:

June 3, 1986
Dear Mary and Kevin,
David did not want me to write this letter. But at this stage in life, we can't afford to lose good friends like you who have been part of our lives for more than twenty-five years without at least making an effort to keep them. [3] And besides, I am tired of always saying we've already made plans when you call us.

David and I have been dodging the truth for years. But you just called us again, and I want to stop pretending that everything's fine because it's not! [1] I'd like to make things right so we can be friends again, but I need your help. [5 and Ask for a specific response]

Remember six years ago when the four of us invested in that rental property? We agreed to be equal partners, but after that, there were lots of monthly maintenance costs and David and I have paid all of them.

David is too embarrassed to ask you for the money.

And I've been too angry to bring it up before now—so that's why we've stopped doing things with you. [Pinpoint the problem without blaming] What a waste! I miss our late night bridge games and our Sunday morning crossword puzzle brunches, too. [4] I want all of us to get back to being friends like we used to be. I miss both of you, and even though he won't admit it, so does David. [2] How can we settle this? Any ideas? [Ask for a specific response]

Love,
Suzanne

✦ Her Two-Sided Message

Below you will find a powerful message from a woman about unspoken resentments that were coloring her relationship with her brother. The *Pinpoint the problem without blaming* element is reflected in her words "I feel closed out of your life and hopeless to do anything about it." She also asked for a specific response: "how about recording some of your thoughts and mailing this tape back to me?"

Using both sides of an audiocassette tape, the woman recorded her thoughts and feelings. Then she mailed the tape to her brother.

Here is what she wrote on side A of the tape's label:

Side A: November 1998
Steven, Listen to This Side First

Below is the message this woman recorded on side A:

Steven,
I am using every single bit of courage I have to let you know that I miss the kid brother I used to have. I miss the feeling that if all hell broke loose and my life got out of control, I could turn to you and that if things were reversed you could turn to me. [3] Now that we're both old married people, it seems like there's a wall between us—especially for the last eight years.

Sometimes I feel mad at you and hurt because I feel closed out of your life and hopeless to do anything about it. [Pinpoint the problem without blaming]

I am telling you this in a tape recording so I can keep erasing my words and practice changing the tone of my voice until I sound friendly and truthful—because that is how I do feel about you. [2]

I might have kept on acting as if things are fine except that last week your wife mentioned something that made me wish I could straighten a few things out. [1] Diane said you wondered how, coming from a family like ours, you still had a sense of what to do in order to be a good father to your son. You told Diane that, even though your early years had been terrible, someone must have nurtured or loved you enough for you to know how to love your own child now.

Well, I remember that someone did love you very much when you were small. [4] I know for a fact that it wasn't your alcoholic stepfather or your self-absorbed mother! It was that little girl who lived in your home—me! And OK, I guess there were lots of times when you resented me for telling you what to do and lots of times that I did a poor job of "mothering," but since I was only two years older than you were, I did the best I could.

I'm telling you this because if you are going to be angry at me because I was bossy in the past, then, maybe you could factor this in, too: All that I want for now is to have you in my life as my good friend! I miss you. [5]

Here is the label she put on side B of her tape:

Side B:
Steven, Never Mind
Since this side of the tape is blank, how about recording some of your thoughts and mailing this tape back to me? [Ask for a specific response]

❥ *If We Stay Together*

Here you will find two messages about conflict and anger. Although these messages address a married couple's struggle to survive an infidelity, the same elements apply to messages about other difficult and painful issues that can rip couples apart, such as alcoholism or bankruptcy.

In this letter, an angry and distraught woman used writing in the margins to release some of her pain in order to create a heartfelt message that is free of blaming words.

Notice, in particular, how difficult (and ultimately how effective and important) it was for this sender to apply basic elements 2, 3 and 4 in her message. Her margin notes show you how she struggled to include these elements in her letter.

Her written purpose shows the sender's determination to find and focus on her positive intentions.

> The gift I want to give you in this message:
> When I think about the future, I guess it could go
> either way, but I really want to find a way to trust you
> again and if you want this, too, I am willing to look for
> ways to work this thing out.

The sender went through five drafts before she created the message you are about to read. Below is her final version along with the thoughts and feelings that came up in her as she worked on her letter:

What She Wrote:

What She Was Thinking:

January 1995
Dear S.,
You just left for work and I am still sitting here hurt and confused and trying to figure out how to save our marriage. [1] The problem is I am having a lot of trouble trusting you. [Pinpoint the problem without blaming] I want to get past this because it feels awful. But how do people get over anger as big as this?

How could he do this to me? I hate him, but I love him. It's making me crazy.

I don't know if I'll ever trust him again.

You've apologized and promised it will never happen again. Still I feel hurt, angry and suspicious. I'm stuck between wanting to move on and forget it ever happened and wanting to punch you or hurt you to get even. I want to do both of these things! Crazy, I know, but that's how I feel. I remember so many special things we've shared and I know that I must love you a lot to be this angry—or else I'd hang it up right now. [2]

I'm scared to leave but I could move in with my sister for a while.

When I think about the future, I guess it could go either way. Making a life without you would be sad and scary but not impossible. I would miss your ability to be silly and the way you bring that out in me. [3] You

Did you make that other woman laugh, too? Will I ever get the image of the two of you out of my mind?

have managed to teach me not to be so serious all the time. [4] This, however, is not one of the times when I can stop feeling serious. Maybe someday, not today, though.

Today, just knowing that I could leave and make it on my own lets me feel willing to wait this out for now. That's weird I guess but true. Also true, is this: I really want to find a way to trust you again. [5]

If I can...

If we stay together, we are going to have to find new ways to talk to each other. I am so tired of the crying and yelling and silent treatment that, for now, I think we should write letters to each other. Would you be willing to write back to me? [Ask for a specific response] Maybe that would help us.

E.

I hope we can stay married, but now I'd be happy just to stop yelling at each other.

At least we can't scream in a letter.

This is her husband's response. We wanted to show you his letter because it seemed to us to be an example of the kind of positive response that effective messages—even those created in the midst of great emotional upheaval—can often generate:

January 1995

Dear E.,

Thank you for writing to me. I want to make things right between us, too. God, I feel so awful. I know you are angry and I don't blame you for that. This is a mess and no matter how much I say I'm sorry, I don't know what else to do. I just don't know how to fix this.

I miss the way we used to be before I screwed up. I'm tired of all the arguing, too. I know we are at a make-it-or-break-it place. I don't want to lose you, but I don't think I can stand things the way they are now.

A guy at work told me his marriage ended when he messed around. His wife just walked out and never looked back. That was five years ago and he's still upset and blames himself for everything he lost.

I will do anything to keep that from happening to us. I'll write more letters, I'll go with you to see a marriage counselor, or anything else you can think of to prove that you can trust me and that I am sorry and that I love you.
    S.

11

Your Family Matters

$\mathcal{F}$amilies look and operate differently today than they did in years past. Divorce rates are high, blended families (step-families) are increasingly common and so are single parent homes. The messages in this chapter address some of the issues and pressures that affect family life today.

These messages may or may not have been kept as treasures by the recipients. Remember, it's the eye of the beholder that ultimately determines whether or not a message is so special that the other person keeps it. However, what seems most important to us about the examples here are the ways in which the basic elements and the techniques of Putting your purpose on paper and Writing in the margins helped each sender get his messages across.

These messages encompass touchy subjects such as fears for new teen drivers, worries about eating disorders, discomfort with current fads such as body piercing, the fallout from a divorce and the long-term effects of adoption.

As different as these messages are from one another, all of them used the basic elements to express positive intentions even when the sender was feeling anxiety, anger or discomfort.

❧ *Driving Dad's Message Home*

We think the message below does a great job of combining love and concern with practical advice in an original (and hard-to-ignore) manner. When the single father of a boy who'd just gotten his driver's license told us the following story, we asked his permission to share it with you here. This is what he told us:

James is a really good kid. But the fact is he's only sixteen years old and that means that he makes sixteen-year-old decisions. The idea of my son out there driving on any road, at any hour, in any car—no matter how safe a car I put him in—was making me a wreck. So, before I let him take the car out by himself I sort of "modified" it and put in some safety messages that he couldn't possibly overlook. I started by putting my purpose on paper.

The gift I want to give you in this message:
A reminder to be careful when you drive so you will be
safe, which is important because I love you.

After that I was ready to begin. Just above the car radio, I put a note that I'd written. The note was about the size of an index card. I had a local printing shop laminate it for me, then I glued it in place. This is what my note said:

> February 8, 1999
> Dear James,
> Because you are a new driver [1] and because I love you [2], I want you to be safe.
>
> I'd like you to drive without the distractions of loud music, [5]. I've been in the car with you often enough to know that you love switching radio stations and blaring the music. I still remember how we laughed when you found out I thought your favorite rock group was called In-the-Sink instead of 'N Sync. [4] You have worked hard to make me a lot more hip! [3]
>
> But son, I'm worried that until you have more experience as a driver, that you might lean over to crank up the music and take your eyes off the road, and that's how accidents can happen.
>
> So, if you can drive for a whole year without getting a single traffic ticket, then you are looking at the spot where I will install a brand-new CD player with all the special features you want.
> Love,
> Dad

You know those drink holders that come in cars today? Well, I took a soft drink can and on it I pasted another note and a picture of a friend who had died. Then I set the can right into the drink holder. Here's what that note said:

Drinking and driving is deadly. You're a new driver. This
reminder is brought to you and your passengers by your
dad, who loves you and will never forget that his own best
friend (your godfather) was killed by a drunk driver.

*The last modification I made was on the key ring I gave to James. Besides
the house and car keys, I added two small hole-punched, laminated cards
(about the size of a business card). One of the small cards said:*

I love you. I trust you to drive with your full attention on
the road at all times. If you are ever unsure of your ability
to do so, all you have to do is call me and—no questions
asked—I'll play taxi driver to you and your friends.

The other card I put on his key ring said:

If an accident happens, and it probably will, we'll deal with
it together. You don't have to be a perfect person. Nobody
is. You do have to try to be a perfect driver. Your life de-
pends on it.

*At first, my son was embarrassed by all the stuff I glued into his car. He
was mad at me, too. But now that his girlfriend is about to get her driver's
license, James is making a bunch of notes like mine to put inside her car.*

❧ *You Want to Pierce Your Tongue? Yuck!*

Whether it's long hair on boys, breathtakingly mini skirts on girls, too-
tight pants, torn jeans or purple hair, teenagers seem to delight in creating a
look that shocks us. But what if what your teen wants to do is unhealthy? That
is what this letter from a mother to her seventeen-year-old daughter addresses
effectively by adding in all the basic elements:

June 1999
Dear Jenny,
I guess it's a good thing that being a parent isn't a popularity contest because after saying no to you about piercing
your tongue, I figure Dad and I rank somewhere below
toilet level with you. [1] Nevertheless, you do not have our
permission to pierce your tongue and here's why:

1. I met some professional singers who told me about a
   girl who'd had her tongue pierced and ten days later
   was unable to speak because an infection from the

piercing traveled through her system and destroyed the lining of her trachea and larynx.

2. Another man (midtwenties) who was a member of the resident opera company told me that he'd had his lip pierced three years ago and then he was unable to perform for four months, also because of an infection.

3. Do you remember when you had your belly button pierced? [4] It makes me smile when you do something so independent and zany [3], but you developed an infection—so obviously you're susceptible to physical problems.

While it is true that I think piercing eyebrows, lips, tongues and noses is gross, I accept that kids today like that look. Our decision to say no is not about what I consider pretty. Our decision is based on our love for you and a real concern about your health. [2]

Now that I know about the dangers, there is no way I can give you permission to pierce a part of your body that is connected to soft internal tissue.

I know we might not be able to stop you, but as people who love you with all our hearts, we hope you'll forgo piercing altogether or at least puncture a part of your body that puts you at less risk. [5]

Love,
Mom

✦ *The Weight of Their Words*

Eating disorders (anorexia nervosa, bulimia, bingeing and purging) are often upsetting, even life-threatening diseases that afflict as many as one out of every one hundred people living in industrialized societies like ours—where beauty is linked to thinness. Although doctors tell us that a growing number of boys suffer from these disorders, girls between the ages of thirteen and twenty are most at risk. That can be scary news if you're a parent of a teen daughter.

Can a mother and father share their fears about a deadly illness and actually get through to their child? How can they get past their child's rock solid conviction that there is no such thing as too thin? And what can they possibly say that will impact an adolescent who, like the majority of teenagers, has no sense of her own mortality?

We learned some answers to these questions when we came across the next message written by a mother and father to their teen daughter. It seems to us that when both parents are willing to address their child's tough issues, such as eating disorders, addiction or other potentially destructive behaviors, together, their words are more likely to get through. And when parents support one another during times when the going gets rough (and it does), they are less likely to be manipulated or played one against the other.

The parents whose message you are about to read said they had tried everything they could think of to reach "Lauren," but all their attempts to talk with her had produced only shouting, denial and door slamming.

Here is how her parents described what led them to create their message:

Lauren had lost a lot of weight very quickly. When we listened carefully, we noticed how often she was complaining about her body and calling herself fat or disgusting. Also, no matter what we served, she just picked at the food and hardly ate, and as soon as the meal was over she raced to the bathroom.

We were really worried about her, but when we tried to talk with her, it didn't go very well. We talked to several doctors and finally we just had to face the truth: Lauren seemed to be suffering from a disease that strikes thousands of teenage girls in this country every year and kills almost 15 percent of them.

We love Lauren. We just couldn't sit by and watch her suffer from a disease that could end her life. So we had her evaluated by a physician, and then, following the doctor's recommendations, we had Lauren admitted to an inpatient eating disorders treatment program.

She fought us every step of the way and screamed at us, claiming we were interfering with her right to control her own body and appearance. But we had to get some help. We are two parents who love our daughter and felt as if we had to act responsibly in spite of her rage. We could not bury our heads in the sand.

When we wrote this letter, Lauren had been in treatment for two weeks. Her counselor said Lauren was angry and that she refused to talk with us in person or by phone. Instead, the counselor suggested that we write Lauren a letter. Using the Putting your purpose on paper technique and the basic elements of a special message, we made our way through a lot of torn-up paper before we put together a letter that said what both of us felt.

Lauren's parents began by putting their purpose on paper.

The gift we want to give you in this message:
To let you know we love you and will do anything we
can to help you live a happy, healthy life.

Here is part of their letter (to insure their privacy, we have omitted some portions):

November 1998
Dear Lauren,
We have had you in our prayers every moment you've been in the hospital. [1] We are writing this together to let you know that we love you without reservation and that we will do whatever we can to help you live happily and healthily. [2]
    This is not the first time that our family has had to pull together in order to get through a tough situation. The hardest time was probably six years ago when you told us about what Uncle Joey had done to you. You were brave then and we got through a terrible time because we learned how to tell each other the truth. [3] More than anything else, we are still committed to keeping you safe. That is the most important thing in the world to us. We got through our troubles in the past and we will get through this, too. [4] Our family is tough!
    We know we have a lot to learn about what causes eating disorders and how people recover. That's why we are thankful there are professionals who can help us. So far, we've met with two counselors at the rehab hospital, and they made it very clear that anorexia is a problem that we face together as a family.
    After meeting with the counselors last week, we talked about how we've done things that might have contributed to your eating disorder. After all, you live in a home with a mother who has dieted all her life and a father who points out and admires the beautiful thin women we see on TV and in magazines. Now we realize that our behavior needs to change, too. While you are in the hospital, we are working on making changes so that when you come home you will know you can count on us for appropriate kinds of support and love.
    Darling, when your hospital treatment is over, we'll be right there waiting to hug you, and then we will all work together to become a healthier, smarter family. [5]
    Love,
    Mom and Dad

One of the many things that may have helped this message get through is the way Lauren's parents revealed (in a loving and direct manner) their personal worries and their commitment to change. Another aspect of this letter that makes it especially effective is Lauren's parents' use of the What do we remember and treasure about our times together? element 4 to refer to past problems that they've overcome together. Recalling past successes is a good way to encourage people to keep moving forward, and it lets them know you recall and believe in their ability to do so (element 3, What makes you special to us?).

We also liked the way Lauren's parents referred to their daughter's eating disorder as a family problem. By choosing not to lay blame on any one member of the family, they make it possible for all of them to participate in the healing process.

We've noticed that when parents jointly create heartfelt messages (especially about problems their children may be unwilling to discuss), their positive intentions are more likely to get past their child's resistance and strong negative feelings. And that is exactly what happened in this instance.

❧ *What This Father Never Said*

Some messages help us understand the underlying tensions or strains in our relationships. This one reveals a father's unspoken struggle to be openly affectionate with his grown son.

Partly because this man expressed himself using his true voice ("I thought if I wrote them down now and then worried about how to show you this later, I might get somewhere"), his message rings true. The sender's true voice is particularly apparent and effective when he uses element 5 (*What do I want you to get from my message?*): "This is hard to say but I don't want you to wonder if you were important to me. You are and you always will be, even if I never find a way to tell you this in person." Here is his letter:

> October 1998
> Dear Son,
> You just left after visiting with us for three days. [1] I
> watched you give your mother a warm hug good-bye. I
> tried to hug you, too, but I sort of turned it into our regu-
> lar handshake. I wish I was better at showing you that I
> love you and I'm proud of you. But when I try to say some-
> thing like that, I freeze. Shaking your hand or patting you
> on the shoulder is about the best I can do. I don't remem-
> ber a time when my parents talked about their feelings so
> maybe that's why I don't know how to talk about mine.
> This isn't an excuse but it does explain something about
> me.
> It's funny to be me, living in a time when people talk

about "your inner self" or "emotional release." I don't get what those words are supposed to mean. I understand words like "an honest day's pay" and "a stiff upper lip."

I know your mother wishes I were better at sharing my feelings, but I don't know how. I thought if I wrote them down now and then worried about how to show you this later, I might get somewhere.

When you're not around, it's a lot easier for me to think about how I feel about you. I remember when you protested against the war and put yourself in danger because you felt so strongly about the unfairness you saw. [4] I never told you I was scared and proud of you at the same time. But I was. I still am.

You've gone on to study things that I'll never understand. In fact, I feel confused and sort of stupid when you tell me what you're doing. I wish it made sense to me but it doesn't, so I just stay quiet. I know you're good at what you do, though, and when you're not around, I brag about you to my friends. [3]

Look, I know that we don't have much in common. You try to understand why things are the way they are and then find a way to change some of them. I just accept things without question.

I guess we don't have to be alike for me to be proud of the man you've become. [2] I just am.

This is hard to say but I don't want you to wonder if you were important to me. You are and you always will be, even if I never find a way to tell you this in person. [5]

Love,
Dad

❧ Listening to Love

During the latter stages of writing this book, we found ourselves in conversation with a newly divorced man. When "Roger" learned what we were writing about, he told us about an audiotape he had recorded for his four-year-old daughter, "Betsy":

I wanted to give the tape to Betsy so she'd know that even though I wasn't living in the same house with her anymore, I still loved her and that I always would. Your options are pretty limited when you try to explain divorce to a four-year-old. My plan was to make a tape so she could listen to my voice whenever she wanted to. I hoped the tape would reassure her.

When Roger gave his tape to Betsy, he made sure she had a made-for-young-children cassette player and an extra set of batteries. Betsy's reaction to this tape was so positive that Roger went on and created a series of audio messages for his daughter that now span several years. All together, his tapes have formed a remarkable collection of special messages. Roger's idea seemed so simple and effective that we wanted to share it with you here.

Here's how Roger began. He wrote the date on the tape's label. Then he used an ordinary tape recorder to capture between five and ten minutes of his thoughts. Roger instinctively applied the basic elements of a special message to frame his words. We thought you might like to see what he said in his first message for Betsy:

> Hi, Betsy, this is your daddy.
> I made this tape just for you because I love you very much and I absolutely positively always will. [2] You know what one of my favorite things about you is? The way you love to help me make up new stories. You have a great sense of imagination [3], and you know what? You can listen to this tape over and over again any time you want to. Then, maybe you can imagine that I am right there with you any time you want.
>
> You are on my mind now because I just noticed that soon it will be Sunday, our day together. [1] Hooray! Even though we don't live in the same house anymore, I'm still going to take you out for our special father-daughter Sundays. [4] And just like always, we'll start by eating breakfast at the deli where I will read the Sunday funnies to you while we eat. Then, we'll go to the movies or Grandma's or roller-skating. You choose.
>
> I am going to call you every night on the telephone after dinner to find out what you did during the day. I am going to tickle your chin and call you my Betsy Tickle Head always. I am never going to stop loving you and neither will your mommy. [5]
>
> I know you don't understand why we live in different houses. I don't know how to explain it to you now, but your mommy and I will always try to answer any questions you have about this.
>
> For now, what we both want you to know is that our living in different houses has nothing to do with how much we love you. Sometimes, mommies and daddies just cannot live together. But your mommy and I will always love you. Nothing in the whole world will ever

change that.

Now little Betsy Tickle Head, I send you a great big hug and a promise that I will make another tape recording for you to listen to next week if you like this one. On the next tape, I will tell you a story I've made up about "Silly Annie and Her Five Magic Ponies." Would you like that? I will call you after dinner and you can tell me what to name the five ponies. OK?

See you later, Tickle Head.

We think that Roger's tapes are an effective and loving way of giving age-appropriate information and reassurances to his child. Another thing that impresses us about this tape is Roger's mention of his ex-wife in a positive light.

We hope that if you or someone you know is worried about the impact of divorce on a young child that you will find something helpful in this approach.

❧ Communicating for a Greater Good

The message below is an e-mail that was sent by a recently divorced man to his former wife. While it's unlikely that the woman who received this message felt as if she'd received a special keepsake, we have included the man's e-mail here because it is a good example of how the basic elements of a message can help people communicate effectively even in turbulent times.

In this case, the man's message was sent to bridge the distance between him and his ex-wife so that they could communicate regularly and raise their children together in greater harmony. Here's the e-mail message:

Date: June 21, 1998
To: Caroline
From: Jack
Subject: For the Kids' Sake
Dear C.,
Our final divorce papers came today, and I'm worried about the effect all this will have on the kids. [1] I don't want our bitterness to spill on to them, and I'm pretty sure that you feel the same way.

You know, lately it has been easy to think about all the bad things that happened between us. But I remember good things, too, like that time when we took the kids to Disneyland. [4] Remember the way you invented rhyming games to keep us from killing each other while we waited in those endless lines? I do. I remember thinking that you were the most creative and patient mother I had ever seen. [3] I still think that. [2]

I also still think that you and I worked well together when it came to being good parents. We did a good job of keeping the lines of communication open.

I was thinking about all that and wondered how we can continue to find ways to keep each other up to date about what's going on with the kids. I thought that e-mailing each other might be a good way to do some of this. So I'm going to e-mail you each time the kids spend the night at my house so you will not be left out of the loop on anything important that might have happened.

I'd like it if you would e-mail me about any things that pop up when the kids are with you that you think I should know about. That way we can still be the kind of parents our kids deserve. [5]

I would like us to continue to present a united front to Alison and Charlie. I think that will help keep them from doing what a lot of kids whose parents are divorced do—which is to try to play one parent against the other. And if you have other ideas about how we can work together, I'm open to your thoughts. I believe both of us want to make sure that our kids aren't hurt too badly by what has happened between us.

Thank you,

J.

➤ Where's William?

In cases where joint custody is awarded, adjusting to living in two different homes can be really difficult for children. Here is a message made by a mother to help her ten-year-old son adjust to spending every other week in a different home.

Besides applying the basic elements, this note does some things so extraordinarily well that we want to point them out to you here. Early on, Will's mother makes it clear that she has noticed sadness in her son. Then, she puts herself in his position and tells him that she'd feel that way, too. Identifying with another person's feelings seems to help that person feel understood and accepted. And, doing so also tends to relax the receiver, allowing him to be more open to the words that follow.

In her third paragraph, she reminds her son about another time when he faced a similar challenge and overcame it superbly. That struck us as a wonderful way to help someone know we believe in his ability to succeed. We think that the way Will's mom applied element 5 (*What do I want you to get from my message?*) at the end of her message was particularly generous. She aligned herself with her former husband in the most positive light with her words "What

I want you to get from my letter is this: How you feel is important to me and to your dad. We want you to share your feelings with us." Below is the complete letter:

March 1999
Dear Will,
I know we've talked about how much your father and I love spending time with you. Since the divorce, we made sure we both live in homes that are near your school so you can spend one week here with me and then the next week with your dad.

But the other day, when I was packing the clothes you'd need for your week at your dad's house, I thought you looked sort of sad. [1] I'm worried about how moving back and forth between two houses might be affecting you. I think if I was living in two different homes that I'd probably feel lost or confused for a while.

But then I remembered another time when you looked sad as you watched me packing your clothes. That was a couple of years ago when you were heading off to overnight camp for the very first time. [4] Remember how scared you were? I thought you were really brave [3], and I was thrilled when you came home and told me it had been the best summer of your whole life.

I was proud that you were willing to try new things and make new friends. You sure came through that with flying colors. I think you're pretty cool. [3] Another thing I think is that once we all get used to this moving around stuff, we'll be the coolest divorced family ever.

Until then, things will probably seem confusing. I was looking for a way to make this easier when I saw your old *Where's Waldo?* book. It gave me an idea that I thought might help.

I made a monthly calendar called Where's William, and on it I put your school information, including your band practices, field trips, etc. Then I circled the weeks you will be staying with me in blue and the weeks you will be staying with your dad in red. I made copies of this for you, Dad, Grandma and me so all of us can always know where in the world you are.

Will, as you know, Dad and I don't agree on everything, but we do agree that we want you to be happy. I know that this is not how you wanted things to work out.

None of us did. But what is most important (and will
never change) is how much we love you. [2]

What I want you to get from my letter is this: How
you feel is important to me and to your dad. We want you
to share your feelings with us. [5] So as we go along, we
hope you will tell us how things are going for you. OK?
See you Sunday, Will.

I love you [2],
Mom

❥ As Long as She's on This Earth

Inside the front cover of a book called *Inventing Memory*, written by Erica
Jong, a grandmother inscribed a special message for her seventeen-year-old
granddaughter. The young woman who received this message told us her
grandmother's message helped her believe that she'd be fine even though her
family seemed to be falling apart.

We really liked the way "Grandma Joan" expanded on element 3 (*What
makes you special to me?*) by mentioning some of the wonderful qualities she
had observed in her granddaughter: "I realized you've become a remarkable,
caring and insightful young woman whom I'm delighted to know."

Here is the inscription she wrote inside the book she sent to her
granddaughter:

> December 1999
> My darling Jessica,
> You were on my mind the whole time I read this book, so
> I decided to send it to you. [1] This is the story of four
> women who, in spite of all that happens to them, manage
> to pass along the best parts of themselves to the next gen-
> eration. Read it and you will know more about my philoso-
> phy of how to get through life's good and bad times.
>
> I have been thinking back over our recent phone con-
> versations and about how upset you've been about the
> fighting that was going on in your home. I was so touched
> that you felt close enough to me to call and share your
> worries. [4] As we talked, I realized you've become a re-
> markable, caring and insightful young woman whom I'm
> delighted to know. [2 and 3]
>
> Jessica, I've lived a lot of years and I've seen many
> things change—some good (like the arrival on this earth
> of you, my precious granddaughter), some not so good
> (like the news that your parents are going their separate
> ways). What I know is that we women are strong and can

handle anything, especially if we have each other to turn to. I want you to know that I am your grandmother and no matter where or with whom you live, I will remain your devoted and loving grandmother. You can count on that to be true as long as I'm on this earth. [5]

Love,

Grandma Joan

❧ No Wars at the Wedding

Even after many years have passed, grown children can continue to be hurt by the bitterness between their divorced parents. "Tina," a high school teacher whose mother and father had divorced nearly two decades earlier, dealt with this issue in a message she mailed to her feuding parents. Here is how she described her dilemma:

Six months before my wedding, I was a wreck from worrying that my parents would pull some stunt or act out their anger toward one another in public and spoil what should be the happiest day of my life. Thinking about that made me furious.

Tina had a practical agenda: She wanted to tell her parents to behave themselves at her wedding. But she believed that getting through to them in a conversation without losing her temper or getting caught up in their ongoing war was unlikely. So, Tina wrote one letter and sent a copy of it to both of them. Her message opened the door and set in motion some much needed healing and reconnection.

She began by putting her purpose on paper.

> The gift I want to give you in this message:
> Some way to make sure there will be no fighting.
> No snarling. No kidding!

Rereading her written purpose, Tina told us the following:

I saw that I was carrying around a lot of anger about how my parents had handled things in the past. I knew that if I really wanted to get through to them I'd have to separate my negative feelings about what had gone on before from my wishes for a more positive future.

I discussed this with my fiancé and he agreed that I should keep trying to reword my purpose. But no matter how much I tried to express my purpose more gently and turn it into a "gift" for my parents, I just couldn't eliminate my longing for the kind of fantasy family life I'd wished about for years. My fantasy was that the three of us would someday be together in a happy time.

Since I couldn't ignore my own wishes, I finally settled on a written purpose that offered all of us a gift. Here it is:

The gift I want to give you in this message:
A way all of us can enjoy my wedding and remember
that we are part of a family that was and is founded
on love.

Then I sat down and wrote my letter. I revised it for days because I was trying to use all the basic elements and I wanted my words to mirror my written purpose.

It wasn't easy. But each revision moved me farther away from sounding like a little girl who was still afraid of her parents' power to embarrass her and closer to a grown woman who wanted to heal past wounds and find ways to function as a loving family.

I'm pleased with my final letter, especially because it got the ball rolling and helped my parents and me find better ways to relate to each other.

Here is Tina's message to her parents:

January 1999
Dear Mom and Dad,
I don't remember the last time that I wrote to both of you in the same letter. I've been working on this one for over a week.

At first, I wanted to write to ask you both to cool it at my wedding. I was worried that you'd get into that thing you two do and then I'd be embarrassed and my special weekend would be ruined. [1] But then I realized I wanted much more than just your promise of good behavior.

Look, I still definitely want you both to behave at my wedding, but I also really want something that goes beyond making sure that my marriage gets off to a good start. I really want the three of us to start out with a happy new beginning. [5]

I remember back when we were a family and did things together. Do you? Remember how we used to make an Easter egg hunt for the neighborhood? [4] Mom, you always came up with great decorating ideas. And Dad, you really got into the spirit of things giving everyone clues at the top of your lungs over that screechy loudspeaker of yours. I loved those times.

I also remember some of the terrible times. But since I still want to get married and re-create the good things that I saw in our family life, I think that means that you did a lot of good things as parents. Those are the things that I want to pass on to the children we hope to have someday.

Over the years, we've distanced ourselves from each other, but in spite of how you feel toward one another, I love you both. [2] And I want both of you to walk me down the aisle at my wedding.

I know that it is usually just the father of the bride who does this, but I want both of you with me as I walk toward the man who will share the future with me. Maybe that's because you raised me to be a freethinking woman. Or maybe it's because I still wish for a time when the three of us can be happy together. Probably it's both of those things.

So I am asking you both to grant me two wishes: first, that you'll come and celebrate my wedding with me, and smile the whole time. OK? And second, that you'll try to make this the beginning of a new way for all three of us to treat each other—with kindness, appreciation and respect.

I love you both so much and I have learned some wonderful things from the two of you that I will carry inside my heart forever. [3] Thank you.

Your wishful and loving daughter,
Tina

❧ Stepfamily Life

The number of stepfamilies in our country is at an all-time high. And the U.S. Census Bureau says that as of the year 2000 more of us will be living in stepfamilies than in nuclear families. But stepparenting is still a role that most people take on without preparation.

Here is a message that incorporates the basic elements, the two special elements that can help you repair a relationship and the technique of Writing in the margins to address some of the challenges facing people who live in a stepfamily. We've included this letter here hoping that it might give you an example of how making tangible messages can help stepfamilies begin to solve some of the problems that are unique to their experience. This letter was sent by a thirty-seven-year-old woman to her fifteen-year-old son and new husband of seven months:

What She Wrote:

What She Was Thinking:

November 1997
Dear Family,
I am writing this because it has been seven months since we became a family and I am worried about how we are doing. [1] Before Richard and I got married, things seemed fine, but lately I feel so much tension mounting up between the three of us and I want us to find a way to turn back into a more loving family. [Pinpoint the problem without blaming]

I will not start off saying, "Dear Richard and Ben." I'll write, "Dear Family," and maybe they'll remember that's what we are instead of warring creatures from hell.

I know we can do this because I remember that before we got married, the three of us would go out and have great adventures. Like when we climbed up the falls and got to the top just in time to see a double rainbow. Remember how we got a tour guide to take our picture and when we got it developed it looked like the three of us were being hugged by those rainbows? Whenever I look at that photo, I know we really love each other. [4]

My happiest day in ten years.

You know those magazines I read that you both call "literati for loony lasses"? The two of you laughing together about my ladies' magazines tickles me. [3] You both make big booming howls that make me smile. And tease me as much as you like, those magazines have taught me a lot of things about how to get a blended stepfamily like ours on better footing. Reading them, I found out that it's normal for families to bicker. Well, we've got that part down pat! Another thing that's normal in a family with teens is that all teenagers need to pull away to develop more independence and all parents need to slow them

When they laugh together about my stacks of magazines, it sounds so funny. Wonder if they know they're bonding when they do that?

We're something called a blended family with all the regular family problems plus other ones that are wearing me down.

down a bit to make safety the number one priority. So, in that respect we're normal, too.

But there are some things that stepfamilies go through that families that have been together from the start don't have to deal with. For example: Ben, you know how when you're mad at Richard and you holler, "You can't tell me what to do. You are not my father"? And Richard, you know how you get all red in the face and pound the table in frustration when Ben says that to you? And you know the way I get all upset and cry when the two of you go at it? That is the kind of stuff that happens in stepfamilies when they are first getting used to each other.

I feel like I'm stuck between them, and I can't choose one over the other. I just can't.

I'm sick to death of all this tension.

But this can't go on. It is eating me up inside and I love you both too much to be put in a position where I feel like I have to choose one of you over the other. I can't do that.

Ben, you have so many qualities that make me proud. I look at you with more and more admiration each day. I am amazed that you can take anything apart that has a motor in it and put it all back together again in a way that makes it run better than it did in the first place. And I love the way you are always adopting some stray animal and helping it find a new home. [2]

Ben used to be my whole life.

And Richard, you make me smile the moment you walk into the room. There's something so sweet about the way you always offer to cook or clean or drive Ben somewhere without me even asking for your help. [2] I've lived as a single parent so long that it never ceases to thrill me that you want to

Richard amazes me.

lighten my load.

We have got to find some way to calm down and get back to the way we were at first. I have run out of ideas on how we can be the kind of family I think we all want to be. So I made an appointment for us to meet with a family therapist on Friday afternoon. I know I should have asked you before I went ahead and scheduled this meeting, but I was worried that you'd try to talk me out of this. Please don't be angry with me. I just couldn't figure out anything else to do, and I really hope you will show up for this appointment because it is terribly important to me. [Ask for a specific response]

This therapist has a good reputation for helping people like us. I got his name from the pastor at our church. Also, my friend Meredith said she and her family went to him and he helped them a lot.

We need to be there by 4:15 P.M. Here are two copies of a map to his office. Ben, you can walk there from school. Richard, you'll have to leave work early that day. I have already told my boss I have to leave early for a doctor's appointment. We're supposed to meet with the therapist from 4:30 till 6. That way we will still have plenty of time to get to the high school on time for Ben's football game.

Thank you both for reading my letter. Our new family and the two of you mean everything in the world to me. [5]

I love you very much, [2]

M. (which stands for loving Mom and happily Married lady)

Don't they get this?

I know I should've asked them first, but I couldn't take the chance they'd refuse.

What if counseling doesn't work?

If we arrive separately, then neither one of them can try and get me on his side before we have our first meeting with this guy.

I hope this works.

The woman who wrote this message smiled when she told us that her letter helped convince her family to meet with a therapist, who helped them learn to talk about the things that were wrong within the family as well as the things that were right.

❥ *A Question of Adoption*

Perhaps because it's a topic commonly featured on TV talk shows, more and more of us are aware of the long-term concerns that adopted people feel. The message below powerfully communicates an experience that we have heard described by many other adults who were adopted as children.

A young man we met named "Gary" recently told us how much he needed answers from his unknown birth parents. He described how it feels to live with missing pieces this way:

> *I've prayed for the chance to know what really happened to me. It's what I want most. Even if everything I find out is terrible, it would be better than not knowing what kind of people gave birth to me, what they are like, whether they are talented, sick, mean, kind or anything else. Right now all I am is one great big question mark.*

When he discovered a Web site where adopted people can leave messages for their birth parents, Gary wanted to post his own message there. Using the basic elements, the two special elements that help people reconnect and the technique of dumping negative or distracting thoughts and feelings in the margins, he created this heartfelt statement about his crucial need for information (to protect his privacy, we have omitted the personal details and specifics of his birth).

What He Wrote:

What He Was Thinking:

February 1999
To somebody I don't know,
I have no name for you, no address,
no picture in my mind of what you
look like on the outside or what kind
of a person you are on the inside. I
wish I did.

Afraid to ask, heart racing,
more afraid not to ask.

When I found this Internet site, I
decided to write down my questions,
and then I'm going to post them on
the Internet. [1]

I'll put the few facts I know about
my birth with this note, and then I'll

pray as hard as I can that God will lead you to see this and answer my questions.

No matter what reason you had for giving me up, everything is OK. I am happy about what you did. [2] I've been raised by the most wonderful mom and dad anyone could have, but I need something they can't give me.

I shouldn't feel empty after all my adoptive family has done for me.

I remember being really glad there was a family that wanted to love me. [4] But I am not like them. Who am I? Why am I terrible at math? Why do I hate spinach? How come I worry about things that no one else notices? Did I inherit some disease that will make me crazy someday? I feel like I'm a cereal box that no one wants to open because they don't know what it's made of.

Oh God, what if my birth parents are mentally ill? Will I be, too?

I've been told that I was adopted when I was very young. I don't re-member my life before I was adopted. Did alcohol or drugs have something to do with why you gave me up? Was I a bad baby that you couldn't stand? I have so many questions.

Maybe they couldn't stand me. Maybe I did something horrible.

I don't want to barge in on your life. But I want to know what I'm made of, and you are the only people who can help me know myself. [3] How can I ever get married or have kids if I don't know my own medical history?

Please, if you're out there, help me!

Please, can you help me? Tell me something—even what your favorite color is. You could post your answer here on this electronic bulletin board and I would feel so relieved.

I want you to know I have had a fine life and I will not trouble you, but I need your help now, please. [5]

Gary

12

Revealing Secrets to Help and Protect

*F*ew of us enjoy sharing the less-than-perfect truths about our families or ourselves. But there are times when unveiling uncomfortable, embarrassing or traumatic secrets can help or protect other people.

We don't want to leave the people we love with important questions unanswered, but some things are just too difficult for us to say out loud right now. Finding ways to address these questions in messages that can be sent now or put away for later can bring us lasting peace of mind.

Because revealing secrets can an enormous impact on others, it's important to think about the consequences that knowing some information might have on people. The decision to air a secret is not an opportunity to unburden our guilt about things that can only hurt others. For instance, confessing a past infidelity in a message would not be a gift to your spouse after you're gone. However, disclosing a secret may be appropriate when doing so could help, empower or protect another person. The woman who told us the following story makes this point best. Here is what she said:

> For as long as I can remember, I've had really horrible nightmares. I was afraid to go to sleep at night. I went from doctor to doctor but none of them found anything wrong. I felt crazy, even suicidal, and the worst part of it was that I couldn't put my finger on any reason to feel this way.
>
> Just by chance, a distant cousin of mine gave me a piece of information about myself that no one else had ever told me! He said I'd been molested by a baby-sitter when I was three years old.
>
> I guess back then, my parents decided the best thing to do was not to discuss it with me. They probably figured I'd grow up and forget all about it.

I'm sure my parents meant well, but I wish they'd told me. If they had, I'd have known what was underneath all this and I could have gotten help a lot sooner.

What to Include in Your Messages

No matter how you put your messages together (in letters, as tape recordings, etc.), there are going to be times—especially when the information you want to share triggers uncomfortable or negative feelings—when it may be difficult for you to stay focused on your desire to help someone else.

According to the people whose messages you'll find in this chapter, the suggestions we've made here helped them reveal their troubling secrets more comfortably. The topics they address range from a couple's choice to die with dignity to a family's history of alcoholism and a mother's wish to protect her children from her own father.

Here is what can make it a bit easier for you to disclose a secret:
- the five basic elements
- writing in the margins
- putting your purpose on paper
- a new special element called *Why I kept this secret*

Another Look at Putting Your Purpose on Paper

Revealing an explosive, long-held secret can be difficult. Sometimes, unveiling a secret can feel unbearably risky. In other instances, you may be suspicious of your own motives for sharing the information. Maybe you are worried that your reasons to reveal are based on a wish for revenge or a need for self-justification. How can you prevent your messy motives from coloring your messages or from paralyzing you altogether?

Putting your purpose on paper can help you move ahead and stay on course. In fact, after you put your positive intentions in writing, looking back over your words is like keeping your eyes on a lighthouse. Your written purpose can guide you safely through a raging storm of negative feelings. The people whose messages you'll find in this chapter found that this technique made it possible for them to overcome their fears of being vengeful, rejected, disbelieved or worse.

One Special Element for Messages That Reveal Secrets

We have found that no matter what uncomfortable truth your message unveils, the person receiving it is likely to wonder why you have not shared the information before now. That is why using a special element called "Why I kept this secret" can be particularly helpful. This element anticipates and puts to rest the kinds of distracting thoughts that occur when people wonder, *Why haven't you told me this before?* Applying this element increases the chances that the receiver will be able to move past this common and unspoken question and be able to focus on the rest of your words. The key to using this element effectively is to explain concisely and truthfully why you have waited until now to reveal this information. Here is a good example of how you can use the *Why I kept this secret* element:

> I felt I should wait until you were twenty-one before contacting you.

This example is even better:

> The reason I waited until you were twenty-one years old before contacting you was that I didn't want to interfere with the life you were entitled to have with your adoptive family.

While both examples incorporate the *Why I kept this secret* element effectively, the even better version more fully explains the sender's reason for keeping the secret until now. When you apply this special element to messages that reveal a secret, the more fully you explain (without justifying, blaming, glossing over or sugarcoating) the truthful reasons you have waited until now, the more likely it is that the rest of your message will get through to the receiver.

✦ *Grant Us Peace*

This letter, from a married couple, shares the deeply moving experience that led them to write living wills. Although it's about something disturbing, we think their message is a loving gift that may spare their children painful future doubts.

Before writing the letter, they put their purpose on paper.

> The gift we want to give you in this message:
> Information that will make it easier
> for you if you ever face
> this situation.

Here is their message:

October 1994

Dear Children,

We have decided that it is time for us to tell you what really happened when Granddad died. [1] We didn't tell you before because you were too young. [Why we kept this secret] Now that you are grown and have become such caring adults [3], we think that knowing this might make it easier for you if you ever have to face this kind of situation yourselves. We also hope this explains why we do not want to be kept alive by machines.

After he'd had his first stroke, Granddad made sure we knew that he didn't want to live if he couldn't talk, eat or move. Remember when Granddad was in his wheelchair and you both took turns pushing him gently around the backyard so he could check on his garden? You were so sweet to him and whenever we remember that, we feel so proud of you. [4]

But later, after his third stroke, the doctors told us Granddad would never be able to get better, so we asked about humane ways to end his suffering. This was hard. Morally we had a lot of questions. Selfishly we didn't want to let him go. But we thought Granddad had a right to decide this himself no matter how we felt. With a doctor in the room, we asked Granddad to blink once for no, twice for yes if he wanted us to let him go. Granddad blinked twice, over and over. His eyes pleaded with us to end his suffering. With terrible sadness we signed a paper to let the hospital turn off his life-support machines.

We want you to know the decision we made about your Granddad so that if either one of us is ever that helpless, you'd know we want you to display the same courage and respect for our wishes to die peacefully that we extended to him. [5]

Lately we've started putting our lives in order. Today we wrote out living wills. Not because we're ill, but because someday we might be and we don't want you to feel guilty or confused about our wishes. We love you very much [2] and trust you to grant our wish if that ever becomes necessary.

Mom and Dad

We included this couple's letter here because it is such a powerful and straightforward example of how to reveal the kind of information that so many of us find difficult to discuss in person.

The couple who wrote this told us that just knowing they'd written it all down and put it in a safe place for their children to find if they needed it gave them enormous relief and peace of mind.

◆ *Don't Be Afraid to Ask for Help*

Here is a message about a secret history of alcoholism. As brief as it is, the man who wrote it used all five basic elements. This letter shows that even difficult topics can be addressed concisely and effectively when you add in all the elements.

The man who wrote this note told us that although he had succeeded in controlling his alcoholism for more than twenty-five years, he wanted to share this information with his son:

> *I've never told him but you just never know if these things are hereditary. It wouldn't be fair to keep my battle with the bottle to myself if knowing about it could help Greg someday. It took me more than a dozen years to admit I was an alcoholic and get into treatment. I don't know if Greg will ever face anything like this or not. I pray that he won't, but I know that if alcoholism ever does show up, then the sooner you get help, the better.*

This is what he wrote:

> July 1997
> Dear Greg,
> I never told you that I'm an alcoholic because I felt embarrassed. [Why I kept this secret] I've been sober since a year before I met your mother, but having alcohol around could still tempt me. I didn't think you needed to know this but I've changed my mind because I saw a TV show that said alcoholism is something you can inherit. [1] So I think you have a right to know what's in your family history. I love you very much [2], and I like the fact that you take good care of yourself. [3] Please watch out for the first sign of alcoholism and be smarter than I was. [5]
> I come from a long line of alcoholics and so do you. By the grace of God, I am a recovering alcoholic. Since my parents died before you were born, you probably don't know they were alcoholics. My father used to smack us when he was high. My mother got drunk every day and sat in her room crying. You'd think that growing up with that, I'd know better than to start drinking myself. But I didn't and I drank myself to sleep every night for twelve years be-

fore I admitted I had a problem.

The minute you think there might be a problem, go for help! I went to Alcoholics Anonymous. I still go to meetings twice a week. You don't have to be ashamed to ask for help. It takes help and prayer to get sober. Then it takes more help, one day at a time, to stay sober. But I think it is worth it because, when you stop drinking, you can feel things again, like the joy I feel with you and your mom. [4]

From your father

❧ *To Keep Them Safe From Harm*

Below are two letters from a single mom to her teenage children. The first letter is her rough draft. The second letter is her finished message. Although this is a woman's effort to communicate information about incest, the same principles and techniques apply to any potentially explosive secret.

She began by putting her purpose on paper.

The gift I want to give you in this message:
You will know that you need to protect yourselves, your
future children and anyone else who might be in
danger from my father.

Then, by writing in the margins and using the basic elements of a special message and the special element called *Why I kept this secret*, this woman made a rough draft of her letter.

Next, she compared her rough draft to her written purpose and when she did that she weeded out some of her angry, demanding and defensive words. Finally, she rewrote her letter and made it sound more like the gift of safety that she hoped it would be.

Here is her rough draft:

What She Wrote:	What She Was Thinking:
March 1997 To my children,	*My hands are shaking.*
I am writing this in case I die before I have a chance to tell you this. [1] I have something terrible to tell you about my father. He is a bad and dangerous man who raped me when I was seven years old.	*I hate that bastard.* *Oh, God, what will they think of me now?*
I remember that you always	*Please kids, please believe me.*

looked so thoughtful when you asked why we hardly ever visited my parents. [4] You are both smart [3] and I could tell you knew I was hiding something. But I didn't tell you this because I was ashamed and afraid you wouldn't believe me (even my own mother didn't believe me when I told her). [Why I kept this secret] It always came down to his word against mine.

But I can't take this secret to my grave because you might get hurt if I did and I couldn't stand that. I couldn't stand it if he did anything like that to you. I also don't want you to put your own children in danger.

Don't trust anybody in that house!

One other thing you should know is that your grandma won't protect you or your children any better than she did me.

I need you to think about what I've just told you. You've got to believe me and do something to protect yourselves, your future children and anyone else who might be in danger from my father. [5]

I'm sorry they have to know this.

I've made a copy of this letter for your Aunt Susan. She knows what happened to me, and she knows it's true. She will help you. She would love to have you live with her family if I can't be here to raise you myself, and I would like you to live with her, too.

I love them, and I'm scared for them.

I love you dearly [2],
Mom

Notice how in her finished letter (below) this woman was able to adjust the tone of her message using words and phrases that reflected her original purpose. Here is her completed message:

March 1997
To my children,
I was thinking about what might happen to you if I ever

got sick and couldn't take care of you myself. [1] Then, I would want you to know the real reason that I kept you away from your grandfather. I'm afraid knowing this will upset you, but I'm telling you this because it's the only way I can think of to help keep you safe. The truth is that my father raped me when I was seven years old and he kept doing that until I was old enough to move away.

I know you were mad at me for keeping your grandfather out of our lives. I would have felt the same way if I were you. You asked me about this over and over again, but I just couldn't talk about it. I remember that you always looked so thoughtful when you asked why we hardly ever visited my parents. [4] You are both so smart [3], and I could tell you knew I was hiding something. But I was too ashamed and I was afraid you wouldn't believe me because my own mother didn't believe me when I told her. [Why I kept this secret] It came down to his word against mine.

But I can't take this secret to my grave. I'm afraid if I do that, your grandfather might hurt you, and I love you too much to keep quiet and let that happen. I hope that knowing the truth will keep you out of harm's way.

You are the most precious parts of my life, and I want you to know this so that you never let my father near your own children. Sadly, I believe that your grandmother wouldn't protect you or your children any better than she did me.

I am so sorry if this information is disturbing or painful to you. But I had to tell you so you'd be safe if I am not around to take care of you. Please think about what I've just told you and protect yourselves, your future children and anyone else who might be in danger from my father. [5]

I've made a copy of this letter for Aunt Susan. She's the only one who knows all about what happened to me, and she knows it's true. She has my permission to answer any questions you might have about this. Also, Aunt Susan and I both hope you will decide to live with her if I cannot be here to raise you myself. Please take care of yourselves and each other. I love you so much [2],

Mom

We think one of the things that makes this message especially effective is the way the writer acknowledged her children's feelings and point of view.

Using the words "I would have felt the same way if I were you," she removes any guilt her children may have about their feelings or behavior in the past. That, in and of itself, is a wonderful gift.

✦ *His HIV Status*

This is a poignant message from a young man named "Frank" to the parents he hadn't seen in several years. His letter is one of the most touching messages we've seen. Although it could have been included in the chapters about repairing relationships, family matters or comforting others, it made more sense to us to put it here along with other messages about troubling secrets.

Frank created his message by incorporating the basic elements and the new *Why I kept this secret* element by putting his purpose on paper and by writing in the margins.

Here is what Frank told us about his reasons for writing to his parents:

When you get this close to the end of your life, what matters is the connections you have with your family and friends and the chance to say good-bye cleanly.

I knew this might be the last time my parents would ever hear from me. I wanted to let them know that I love them, and I wanted to lessen whatever guilt they might feel about our disagreements and conflicts in the past.

Frank started out with a written purpose.

The gift I want to give you in this message:
Something you can look at to remind you that I love
you and that will give me a chance to say good-bye with
fewer loose ends between us.

Below is the letter that Frank wrote to his parents. He did not include his margin notes in the version he sent to them; however, we left them in here so you could see how Frank managed to keep his negative feelings out of the way as he constructed this remarkably powerful and positive message:

What He Wrote:	What He Was Thinking:
December 1998	
Dear Mother and Dad,	*It is going to hurt them. I hate this.*
This is my sixth attempt to write you.	
I know it will be hard for you to read	*Why did I wait so long?*
this letter. I wish I could tell you this	
in person, but I am too ill now and too	

afraid to look you in the eyes when you learn that I am in the advanced stages of the AIDS disease.

I had to write this because I couldn't come to the end of my life knowing that I'd left you with all kinds of questions about where I've been and why I've stayed away from you and the rest of our family for all these years. [1] I will always regret that I waited so long to reach out for you. I love you both so very much. [2]

Regret, regret, regret. I wish I could tell them about my lover and how he's helped me through this, but what's the point in doing that now? They don't want to see what they've always denied.

I've known I was ill for three years. I didn't tell you sooner because I had made such a different kind of life for myself and had let so many years go by without even sending you a card that I didn't believe I had a right to your love. [Why I kept this secret] Now, I realize that was foolish.

Funny thing is I always thought there would be plenty of time to re-group with my family. I believed that it was more important to let go of all of you in order to find myself. I don't know if this makes any sense to you. It did to me at the time, but now it seems crazy.

They don't deserve this pain.

What I'm trying to tell you is that the reasons I pulled away from you were not your fault. I am also trying to make sure that you know that despite the years and miles I put between us, I love you now and I always have. [5]

I have had a lot of time to think about my situation. I have gone through the whole anger thing about "why me?" and I've raged at God and everyone else.

Please help me make them know I love them.

I feel tired and sorry for myself and sad.

Lately, I have learned how to pray myself into feeling peace, and I have you to thank for that. You both in-stilled in me a deep sense of spirituality and faith that helps me to feel less afraid of whatever may come next.

Remember when you made me go to Bible school? [4] I gave you a lot of lip back then and bad-mouthed the whole thing. I never did tell you how powerfully what I learned there helped me. Thank you for standing up to me when I was a rebellious teen and for insisting that faith is important. [3]

Strange, the things that I remember.

I hope you will come see me. But I am not certain how much time I have left. So I need this letter to help me say good-bye to you in some way that leaves you feeling at peace and aware that I love you both. I do love you and I am sorry for the years that I cut you out of my life. You were and are good parents. We had some wonderful times together in the past, and those memories are with me now.

Dear God, please give me enough time to see them again

Love,
Frank

13

To Comfort Them

*W*hen life's events leave the people you care about feeling sad, fearful, angry or abandoned, how can you help them? What can you possibly say to comfort them? We believe that acknowledging other's circumstances—and expressing your own fears or concerns for them —can help them feel more connected to you and less alone. In fact, letting others know that you recognize their emotional turmoil and that you feel concern for them may be the most comforting message you can deliver.

This point was made especially clear to us when a woman who'd been hospitalized with a life-threatening illness told us the following:

The night before my surgery, a number of friends and relatives came by to see me in the hospital. I tried telling them how afraid I was but nobody wanted to hear that. They all said things like, "Don't worry about anything. You'll be fine," or, "Why by next week you'll be back out on the tennis courts."

I understood that they loved me and that they were probably just trying to reassure me, but it made things worse. I knew there was a good chance I wouldn't make it through surgery, and no one would deal with that!

Luckily, my last visitor did. She came by after everyone else had left and sat at the foot of my bed. When I said, "I'm scared," she said, "Me, too!"

Her words were so honest and unexpected that I could feel my breath catch, and then I relaxed because at least there was one person who understood and wasn't just pretending.

When the people you care about suffer a loss, it is normal to feel angry, fearful and helpless. That's understandable, but it's also a very difficult place from which to offer comfort.

The messages in this chapter will show you a number of ways to move past your own feelings in order to make tangible messages of support for people who are grieving.

One New Special Element

We have found there is one additional special element called "I won't pretend" that, when incorporated in messages of comfort, can be especially helpful for the receiver. This element lets the other person know that you accept the seriousness of her experience, and it helps you put into words your own truthful thoughts and feelings about the situation.

Using this element allows you to acknowledge the other person's feelings and fears and then to reveal your own concerns. When you do this, you help the other person feel heard, more connected and less alone.

Here is a good application of this element in a message:

> I know you're scared. I am, too.

And this is an even better use of this element:

> I know you're scared. I'm glad you could tell me that. I'm
> scared, too. I keep wishing I could do more for you than
> just listen, but if you need an ear, you've got mine—and
> my heart and prayers, as well.

Whether you put your words in a note, attach them to a poem or tape-record them, as long as your messages of comfort combine the basic elements with the new *I won't pretend* element, they can be remarkably powerful sources of comfort for others.

❥ *A Scrapbook for Stephanie*

Very often a child's earliest experience of loss is the death of the family pet. Finding healthy ways to help youngsters feel their grief and learn that life goes on may be one of the most important gifts we can give them. And that's exactly what this message from the mother and father of eight-year-old "Stephanie" does.

In this example, Stephanie's parents acknowledge their daughter's grief (the *I won't pretend* element). Then they go one step further by creating a special scrapbook to help her mourn the family pet in a concrete way. At the same time, these parents leave open the possibility that Stephanie can love another pet, and they head off any guilt she may have about doing so:

> March 1999
> Dear Stephanie,
> We know you are sad since Trooper died. [1] We are sad and miss Trooper, too. We made this scrapbook for you. See how we put some of our favorite pictures of Trooper in it? We also put a piece of his favorite blue blanket on one of the pages, and on another page we wrote a long good-bye letter to thank him for all the great times we had with him.
>
> Any time you read that letter, you can think about how Trooper used to sneak up under the table trying to get us to feed him "people food" and how cuddly he was when one of us was sick. [4]
>
> Nothing we can do will bring him back. [We won't pretend] But there is a lot we can do to keep him in our hearts. Maybe you'd like to do that, too. We left the last three pages in this scrapbook empty so you can add something about what you will always remember about Trooper. You are so good at coloring [3] maybe you will want to draw a picture of something you remember, or you can write down some of your favorite things about Trooper.
>
> He sure was a wonderful friend, and no matter what other dog we ever get, Trooper will always be special. Today we all feel sad. But someday all of us will probably remember Trooper with smiles instead of tears. In the meantime, we hope this scrapbook helps you. [5]
>
> We love you very much, and we are sorry you feel so sad right now. [2]
> Mommy and Daddy

❧ *It May Comfort You to Know*

This is a message of comfort for adult children. This letter addresses, in a loving and straightforward way, the recent death of the children's father.

A woman who came to one of our workshops showed us this message. She had received it some twenty-one years earlier and explained that, "Periodically, I pull it out and reread it. I don't know why it seems so powerful to me. I thought maybe you could show me what makes it special and why it gives me such comfort."

To answer her question, we made a copy of her letter and showed her the portions in it that reflect the basic and special elements. Here is how the sender used the elements to create a comforting message that has held up for more than two decades:

Bruce, Beth, Nancy and Ellen:
I learned very early in life that there are some "boo-boos" too terrible for a Band-Aid to "make all better." My mother died when I was almost six.

Watching someone you love, a strong hunk of a guy, slowly disintegrate before your eyes breaks your heart. [1] Deep aching sorrow and helplessness become companions. You are all so dear to me. [2] You have been so kind to me over the years. [3]

This must be a difficult...and painfully sad...and confusing time for you. It all seems so senseless...so unfair. [I won't pretend] Why should it be?

If talking is a way in which you feel better, and you would like to talk, I am happy to do that with you. It's been my experience that family and friends tend to focus their attention on the surviving spouse and often neglect the needs of the children who are hurting so. And the children have had little or no experience with death and have great difficulty finding the way. Friends of the children sometimes are at a loss in being supportive because of their same inexperience. They don't know what to do and what to say. They feel uncomfortable with the topic. And so sometimes they do nothing. They have such mixed feelings. They identify with their own parents and feel very uneasy.

It may comfort you to know that I will do my best to be supportive and sensitive to your mother.

I would so much like to give you something very "special" at this time—something with your dad in it—that you may receive comfort from and keep with you. [5]

I remembered that Phil took movies of your parent's twenty-fifth anniversary party. (Remember how much fun that party was?) [4] And so I searched by hand meticulously through reels and reels and reels of films, and finally I found it. I clipped the sections and am enclosing it for you. (I hope they are good. I have no camera in which to view it.)

With affection,
Bernice

❧ *About What Might Have Been*

This e-mail, written by a couple in their fifties, addresses the sadness surrounding their daughter's recent miscarriage. We have included this message here because it uses the basic elements and the new *I won't pretend* element with the words "We wish we could protect you from the hurts and sadness of this time." We also want you to see this letter because we were touched by the thoughtful way this couple acknowledged their daughter's and son-in-law's feelings of loss and sadness.

> March 19, 1999
>
> Dear Kristen and Ted,
>
> Your dad and I just hung up the phone after talking with Ted, who told us about your miscarriage. [1] We love you both [2], and we are so broken up over this. You two are the sweetest young people we know. [3] You are always there helping others—we remember how you jumped on a plane and came here to help out after Dad's last surgery. [4] No wonder when we got off the phone, we wished we were standing right there beside you.
>
> We hate that we live too far away to have been with you when this happened. We have booked a flight and are planning to come spend a few days with you next week. We can stay at the hotel around the corner, or we can stay at your house—you decide which you'd prefer. If you are not feeling up to having us visit this soon, just let us know. Otherwise we're coming to do what parents do—cook, run errands, answer the phone and comfort you as best we can.
>
> We wish we could protect you from the hurts and sadness of this time [We won't pretend], but we're glad you have each other, and we hope you know that you've got us, too. You're in our prayers and soon you'll be in our arms. [5]
>
> Love, Mom and Pop

❧ *All That Matters*

Facing the truth about our own mortality can feel overwhelming. But this letter by a woman in good health with every expectation of a long life shows that acting as if death might happen at any time can motivate us to create powerful messages of comfort and love for those who may outlive us:

May 9, 1988

For my husband,

This is a letter that I hope you won't read for a long time because I want a zillion more years to laugh, cry and love together. But there are a few things I want to tell you in case a time comes when you have to go on without me. [1]

I know that when someone dies, the loved ones left behind suffer guilt. [I won't pretend] They wish they had said something differently or not at all. They remember arguments, plans they delayed or things they should have done but didn't.

I cannot protect you from such thoughts. I can protest, in advance, their absurdity. We lived our lives exactly as we did—in a partnership that represents some of the finest moments of my life. We fashioned our marriage together. I do not regret one single moment. I would not have missed the joys or pains or laughs or disagreements that characterized our time together—not for anything! [4]

Having just celebrated ten years of marriage, I feel lucky to have known your smile, your touch and your love. [3] There is nothing about our lives together that I would change. You were not perfect. Neither was I. We loved each other and comforted each other, and that is what matters. That is all that matters.

If I learned anything during our time together, I think it was to live each day as fully as possible. And that is what I leave behind as a legacy for you and our children. Please go on. Comfort each other, remember me at times but know that I want all of you to love and laugh again. [5] I send you a hug and my love always. [2]

❧ Suicide—Helping Survivors Survive

Despite its frequency, few of us know what to say or how to help a person whose loved one has committed suicide. Often, the people who mourn victims of suicide face not only the anguish of a sudden loss but enormous guilt, anger and confusion, as well.

Sometimes their inner turmoil is made even worse by the social stigma attached to suicide. For many of us, suicide is a subject we would prefer to ignore. Sadly for survivors, the way people react to their grief is often colored by society's harsh judgment. And many times, other people's obvious discomfort heightens a survivor's sense of aloneness.

When people who are dear to you experience the kind of terrible upheaval that a suicide generally produces, experts say that the very best thing you can do is to listen, and listen, and listen. Our own experiences have shown us that it takes a great deal of compassion, time, respect and goodwill to help a survivor heal.

The message below addresses the wrenching pain caused by someone's suicide, and it offers genuine compassion to a woman whose husband of thirty-nine years recently took his own life:

> October 1999
> Dear Julia,
> I am sitting here in my bathrobe—where I've been for over an hour—and I keep reaching for the telephone and then hanging it back up. Julia, I love you very much and I want to call you. I want you to know how sorry I am for all the terrible pain you must be going through since Wayne's death two weeks ago. But I can't find the right words to say, so I'm writing this instead. [1]
>
> I know the two of you had problems, but there is no doubt in my mind that you loved each other very much. I used to watch Wayne light up when you walked into a room. I have heard him tell the story about how the two of you met—so many times that by now I can repeat it myself word for word. I remember helping you shop for his birthday present last year. [4] You are so caring [3] that you took an incredibly long time picking Wayne's gift and the man behind the counter finally had to sit down because his legs were cramping!
>
> I have never suffered the kind of loss you are feeling. [I won't pretend] I never lost someone to suicide. Since I can't begin to know what you are going through, I got three books from the library about how to be a good friend to someone who is coping with the suicide of someone she loves. All three of the books say that the questions a survivor is left with, the agony of thinking that you should have seen this coming and the bouts of anger you feel at the person who's gone are huge.
>
> The books that I read also said all those feelings are normal and that the people who love you can expect that you'll need to talk about this for years and years. Eventually, according to the people who wrote these books, talking to someone who really listens can help you get over the worst parts of this horrible hurt. I want you to know that you can talk to me. I know that reading books doesn't make me any kind of an expert. I can only be me—a

friend who loves you [2] and feels angry sometimes with
Wayne for leaving you.

I hope you won't mind, but I went to a counseling
center near here that is pretty well known for helping survivors of suicide. I went there for me. I wanted to know
more about what you are going through, but I also wanted
some advice about how I can help. The director there
spent over an hour with me. She introduced me to a
woman whose husband committed suicide twenty-five
years ago. That woman told me she's gotten over the terrible parts of her loss, but there are still times when it helps
her to have someone she can talk to.

She also said that after her husband's death, many of
her friends drifted off, and after a while, even the ones
who didn't started saying it was time for her to get on with
her life. She said they acted as if they were tired of hearing
about what she was going through and said most of them
seemed so squeamish about suicide that she felt more
alone than ever.

I don't want to do anything like that to you. I can't
promise that I'll know the right thing to say, but I still
hope you'll call me when you feel like talking.

I bought a copy of one of the books I saw in the library. I thought it might give you some comfort or information about how other people who have been hurt by
suicide got through this. The book is called *No Time to Say
Goodbye: Surviving the Suicide of a Loved One* by Carla Fine.
Her husband took his own life about nine years ago, and
she wrote about it in a way that gave me a better idea of
what you might be feeling now.

I also got a list of some groups they have at the counseling center for people whose spouses have died from
suicide. The woman told me that they also have a twenty-
four-hour telephone number so you can call and talk to
someone who has gone through what you are dealing
with (I wrote the number on the bottom of this page for
you to keep). She said holidays and other special times of
year can be pretty difficult to get through. Since Thanksgiving is coming up in a few weeks, I wondered if you
might like to come with the kids and me to Colorado for
the week. No pressure. Just an invitation to spend time in
new surroundings. There's plenty of room. You'd have the

second story of the house to yourself. You can spend time
with us, go off by yourself or do a little of both. Think it
over.

I decided not to mail this. I am bringing it over to you
now hoping that when you read it you will know what's in
my heart. [5]

Love,

Grace

We think what makes this message a loving gift has as much to do with
what it says as what it doesn't say. This letter offers comfort without platitudes.
It does not ignore the truth about the way Wayne died, and it does not con-
demn his suicide. Instead, the sender's words invite communication when the
receiver is ready.

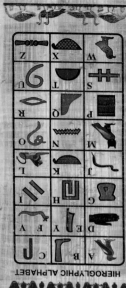

HIEROGLYPHIC ALPHABET

Z	X	W
U	T	S
R	Q	P
O	N	M
L	K	J
I	H	G
F	E	D
C	B	A

King Tut & his Wife

14

Sharing Your Traditions and Life Lessons

*T*hroughout our lives there are certain small moments that happen in a flash and change us forever. These moments are often filled with the lessons that light our way and affect us deeply. Perhaps we've been inspired by what others have done. Maybe our lessons are rooted in our religious beliefs, family traditions or personal values. Wherever our inspirations come from, when we find ways to preserve them and pass them along, we may be able to help other people now and in the future.

That's what this chapter is about—making messages to preserve the lessons we've learned and the traditions we value.

❧ *Her Top Five Values*

Some time ago, a friend of ours told us that she simply didn't believe it was possible to pass along life values to young children except, of course, by example or occasionally engaging them in conversations about right and wrong.

"How can anyone possibly put their values and beliefs and personal morals in a message for children without sounding corny or preachy?" she asked.

Good question, we thought. Looking for an answer, we asked this woman if she would be willing to help us conduct an experiment that we've included here because it seemed to work.

We gave our friend an alphabetical list of nearly one hundred different values (accomplishment, dedication, fame, justice, love, money, perfection, respect, wisdom, etc.). Then we asked her to pick the five values that seemed most important in her life. Finally, we asked her to list the five values she selected, put them in order of their importance and, using the basic elements, write something about the value that she'd put in the number one spot on her list. After several loud sighs and lots of crossing out, here is what she wrote:

> October 1998
> Dear Children,
> I wanted to write to you about my personal beliefs and values. [1] We've talked often about right and wrong and God and prayer. I remember how hard it was for you to understand that there is a God since you can't see God.
>
> I loved what happened when all of you tried to draw your own pictures of God. Do you remember that? Your pictures were gorgeous! [4]
>
> I love you so much. [2] And since you have given me so many moments of joy [3], I'd feel better if I knew for sure I'd given you something meaningful that you could keep and remember for all your lives. So, I wrote down a list of my five most important personal values for you. Here they are:
>
> 1. Humor
> 2. Integrity
> 3. Love
> 4. Health
> 5. Learning
>
> I am surprised that the most important value in my life is humor—and I'm a little embarrassed. I would have preferred to find out that my most important value was something more spiritual or generous. But the truth is that humor has helped me in my life more than just about anything else. I've lost a lot of family members and have been hurt by a few who are still around. My sadness seemed to turn into stories filled with laughter that actually helped me feel better, and telling those stories seems to help other people, too.
>
> So, I guess I'd like you to know how important humor is and has been to me all my life. I'd like you to find the same strength in laughter that I have. [5] In some ways I think I believe laughter is good for the soul, and maybe it's a gift from God to help us cope with our troubles. It's helped me. I hope this letter can help you in the future. I also hope that someday, when you find yourselves laughing your way through a bad time, you'll know that I, too, found doing that to be a blessing.
>
> Love,
> Mom

❥ *It's All Right to Be Wrong*

This is a striking and touching message sent by a seventy-two-year-old father to his eldest son. The man who wrote this had attended one of our workshops, and he told us that using the elements to write to his son had made doing that surprisingly easy.

His letter is about his feelings of love and regret and his hopes that his son and grandson will be able to relate to the people in their lives in a better and more honest way than he did. We think this letter is another wonderful example of how effective it can be to use dialogue in your messages:

> September 1999
> Dear Mark,
> I am sitting on the airplane heading back home while I am writing this. Thanks for inviting me down to go with you to my grandson's big football game. I enjoyed the five days we spent together. I had a wonderful time with you and your family. In fact, watching my grandson play ball reminded me of the old days when you were a high school athlete and I was your proudest fan. [4] As good as you were at sports, you are an even better son, and I don't think I've ever told you that. [2] You have always made me proud. Even when your team lost, you never lost your good nature. [3]
>
> Anyway, one reason I'm writing this is because I can almost hear the words your mother would have said if she were still alive and could have seen the way you and your son argue about things. [1] She'd have noticed that neither one of you would allow yourselves to admit you might not be right. Then she'd have pointed her finger at me and said, "You see that, Scott? The way those two are behaving is your fault! I have been telling you for years that you set a pretty poor example for a boy when you can't admit you're wrong about anything in life. Why do you always have to be right? Now Mark is doing the same thing—just like you and your father and grandfather always did. And now, our grandson is going to grow up believing that men shouldn't be human enough to admit they aren't always right. It's not healthy. It's not true and it gives the people around them ulcers!"
>
> When she was alive, this was an ongoing argument between the two of us. I never did the one thing she'd have liked, which is drop my pride long enough to at least one time tell her that she was right.

I remember many times when I stood in the kitchen with you and demanded that you go along with my way of seeing things. Later on, I'd cool down and be able to see things from your point of view, but I never let on to her or to you.

Now, I am a generation removed, and I watched your son's face when he yelled, "Why do you always have to be right?"

I am not taking sides and I don't want to butt in to your business. Only I do wish that I had taught you what your mom urged me to way back then. I guess I wish I had learned this before now myself. Here it is: I think that one of the best things we can teach our sons is that being a man does not mean that you have to act as if you're right all the time. [5] A grown man can give his son a real gift if he is strong enough to admit that he's not always right and has the courage to say so when it is true. I wish I'd given you that as an example. I am sorry that I didn't show you what your mother knew all along. I think she'd be proud of me for writing this to you, though, and I think she'd be proud of you if you can find a way to help your son know this, too.

I wish I had said all this to you when you were growing up. Then, maybe you wouldn't repeat the mistakes I made. I think you are a good man and a fine father. [2] I am very proud of you. Just remember that to be a good father you don't always have to be right.

Love,
Dad

✦ *An Enduring Ethical Will*

An ethical will is a personal message intended for our survivors and future generations. It can be lengthy or short, taped, handwritten or typed. There is no right or wrong way to make an ethical will. To create one, you look at what has been learned over the course of your life (failures and successes) and include personal decisions about what you believe really counted in the long run.

Below are portions of a powerful ethical will that was written by an acquaintance of ours, Stanley M. Lefco. We have tried to present enough of his wonderful message to show you what an enormously grand gift an ethical will can be. Stan instinctively used the basic and one of the special elements of a message. He wrote about the things he hoped would be important to his children in the future. Every year, Stan adds more to this document. Here is what he wrote on the first page:

For my dear, sweet children,

I began writing this to you in 1995. Most people will never write an ethical will. Most people have never even heard of one. Until recently, neither had I. Then, I read a book about making ethical wills and decided that I wanted to make one for you. [1] I see in you both a great deal of gentleness and concern for many of the things that are important to me. [3]

So, what is an ethical will and why am I trying to write this one for you? My dear and wonderful children, for whom I would sacrifice all if I had to, an ethical will is a document that tells what someone else believes is important in life. It also presents the principles that have guided him. Because I love you both so dearly [2], I am making this ethical will for you to tell you about the things that I believe are important. I hope you will read this often throughout your lives and that it will guide you at times. [5]

I will continue to add to these pages as new thoughts occur to me.

Listen

You do not learn when you are doing the talking. Listen to the world around you and listen to the people. Train yourself to hear what they are saying and how they are saying it. Observe people's body language—how they stand, how their eyes move, what they do with their hands, the expressions on their faces. They are constantly sending out messages. They are telling you what is important to them. Try to be responsive. Your chance to talk will come, if not with that person, then with another.

In life you may find that you are using the word *I* too much. People may seem interested, but they don't want to hear about you all the time. I will repeat this many times. Listen to others. Try not to do what I have been guilty of, which is talking too much about myself. People may be interested, but only up to a certain point. They can tire of you easily. Maybe this is my failing. Ask people about themselves. Find out what they like to do. Their interests will tell you much about them. And it will show that you are a caring person. Listen.

God

I have seen too many good people die and suffer in ways that I find unacceptable. It makes no sense. Yet, as I look around, I see incredible beauty and order in nature, in the flowers, trees, mountains, streams, oceans and wildlife. I have experienced the most remarkable miracle in life: birth—the birth of you, my precious children— and, in that moment, my view of God was clear.

The Stars

On a clear night, look up at the stars. We spend so much of our days and nights looking everywhere but up. Look up. How vast the universe is! How magnificent! It makes me wonder about life, what it all means, and God.

Values

You cannot go through life without a code by which your actions will be guided and directed. We have tried to teach you values: caring for others, being respectful, knowing not everyone has been blessed with the things you have, reaching out to help poor people, not harming defenseless animals and treating others as you would want people to treat you.

Religion

We cannot ask you to be religious. [You decide] But we do want you to study our faith and know it beyond the holidays and its history. Know and follow its ethical and moral standards. You may not be able to follow or accept all its teachings, but many of them are guideposts that I hope you will follow for the rest of your lives.

Family

I lost most of my family before you were born. I don't know anything about them, not even their names. I regret there are no memories to pass on and that their lives ended with their deaths. My father died last year. I know that you remember him. I saw and appreciated how patient you were with him, especially when his health began to fail. [4]

I don't know what kind of relationship he had with his parents. Now, I never will. It's a bit of family history that is lost forever. My dear, sweet children, remember this: I failed to ask the right or enough questions. In most instances I didn't ask any questions at all. I let the history of our family, my life and your life, slip away. I'll always regret that. But you have the opportunity to learn about your maternal grandfather from Mommy and her sister. Don't let the opportunity be lost.

Keep in touch with one another no matter where your careers and other pursuits take you. Talk to one another often, at least weekly. Attend all life cycle events, like marriages, special birthdays and, yes, even funerals. We must be there for one another. Even if we don't know what to say or how to say it, it is more important that we are there. You will always regret the fact that you missed a life cycle event, especially if you do not go because you don't feel like going.

Through you, I have been able to experience what it would have been like to have a brother or sister. Even when you fight with each other, I would have taken that over being an only child. I wish I'd had someone to fight with. You have each other. Always cherish that bond.

15

Messages That Grow Over Time

$\mathscr{P}$erhaps because the speed of our lives, enhanced by almost unimaginable technology, seems faster than ever, there is a growing interest in quilting, scrapbooking, journaling, researching family trees and historical preservation. Maybe the blur of our lives has left us hungry for tangible ways to hold onto what is and was—even as we move toward what will be.

Whatever our reasons, more and more of us are feeling a desire to connect the lessons of our pasts with our actions in the present. And we want to share what we believe—even when our beliefs keep changing—with generations to come.

The people whose messages are included in this chapter found wonderful ways to do just that. Applying the five basic elements, they created touching messages using audio- and videotapes, computer software for researching family trees, and personal journals to frame their evolving thoughts and feelings.

◆ *To Answer His Questions*
Most of us know what it feels like to long for the chance to ask someone who's not here anymore just one more question. And many of us have felt the kind of yearning that accompanies our wish to tell someone who's gone just one more thing.

When a single mom who'd read an early draft of this book told us how she applied the elements of a special message to address these kinds of longings, we wanted to share what she did.

This is what she told us:

When my little boy, Tommy, asks, "Mommy, are you ever going to die?" I say, "Well, someday, but I don't think that will happen for a long, long time—probably not until you are a very old man!" Then I hug him, say good night, turn out his light and shut his bedroom door as quietly as I can.

But after that, I do think. I think about people who aren't here anymore. I think about the things I wish I had asked them, about conversations I never had with them and about conversations I had so long ago that I've forgotten what was said. I hate having questions that can never be answered. I don't even know if the memories I do have are accurate, and I'm really afraid of leaving my son before he has a chance to ask me all of his questions.

So here's how I handle my worries. Every night at bedtime, I take a tape recorder into my son's room. Then, he asks me one question on the tape. Later, when he's gone to sleep, I use the five basic elements to help me tape my answers to his question. In my messages, I tell my son about the things that happened to me and to other people in a way that makes my answers mean an awful lot to him.

My son usually listens to my answer the next morning while he's eating his breakfast. We date and keep all our audiotaped questions and answers. By now there are so many tapes that my son calls them his "library for always." I call them "peace of mind."

Here is what is on one of her many tapes:

> Tommy's question: Today is April Fools' Day, Mommy, so I want to know what tricks you played on people when you were a little girl on April Fools' Day back then.

> His mother's answer: OK, Tommy, I am sitting on the bed in my room now, and I'm looking at some of my old photo albums. I am looking for a picture that will remind me of an April Fools' joke I played on someone when I was little. [1] Your question is a great one by the way. You are a great little "trickster," and I love that about you. [3] You know what else I like about you? Even though you love a good joke, you never do anything mean to other people; your jokes are clever but you always make sure that no one is going to get their feelings hurt when you play a joke on them. Remember when you pretended to be from a foreign country when a substitute teacher came to your class last fall? [4] I'll never forget how the principal and I

laughed when we found out that the substitute teacher had asked that the school assign an interpreter for you!

Oh! I just found a picture of me from the third grade where I've got a great big silly smile on my face and it looks like all my teeth are missing. That is what I did for April Fools' Day when I was in the fifth grade. I put black tape across my teeth just before I went to the dentist for my annual checkup. Boy did that get a laugh from my dentist!

OK, kiddo, I'm tired tonight so I'm going to sleep now. I hope you will like listening to this tape in the morning and that someday you'll make tapes like this for your own little boy. [5] I love you with my whole heart. [2]

❧ *From Russia (With Love)*

Attaching a special message to a family tree before it is passed along can help bring facts alive and turn dry information into vivid communications for generations to come. And when a family tree includes more than names, cities and dates, it can help others connect more fully with their own personal histories, appreciate their family's traditions and understand where they fit into the bigger picture of life.

Today there are literally hundreds of books, Web sites, clubs, magazines and computer programs that make putting a family tree together as simple or as complicated as you'd like it to be. No matter what kind of family tree you may be interested in creating, when you look at the example below, we hope you will notice how adding in little details and attaching a personal note can help you make a touching and lasting gift of the heart.

Sarah, the woman who made this message, told us she is neither an artist nor a writer. But apparently, that didn't prevent her from creating something that, at least to her family, is a treasured work of art. We were impressed with the way Sarah presented her family's history—upheavals and all—without glossing over the events of the past.

Here is the note that accompanied her family tree:

December 1998
Dear Family,
A few months ago, Donny, my very first grandchild, came over to work on his school project with me. Donny has always struck me as a special person, partly because he shows extraordinary kindness to stray animals. Anyway, Donny had to do a report about his family's roots for his fifth-grade class, and he came over to ask me where our family had come from and who some of our ancestors

were. I'm afraid I wasn't much help to him. I remember when his dad was about the same age as Donny is now and looked up at me with the same sweet expression when he had to do the same kind of project for school. [4] I wasn't able to help him at that time, but I promised myself that I would learn more about our family and now I finally have! [1]

I only knew that both sides of our family came to America from Russia because of hardships in that country. I wished I did know more.

So, I bought a computer program to help me make a family tree and I called some relatives who are still around. Then I put this family tree together for all of us. I didn't want our family tree to look like an octopus with a bunch of tentacles leading nowhere, so I put in some things about our relatives to help you know more about them than just their names and birth and death dates.

I would like it if you would add new information to this as our family gets bigger and pass it along to future generations. [5]

I love you all [2] and hope that you'll feel like you know more about yourselves when you take a look at this. I definitely learned a lot about what makes me tick. I always wondered why so many of my siblings dabbled in painting, and I noticed that my husband's side of the family has lots of people who went into politics. I can see things from a long-range perspective now, and it made me feel glad to be able to share this with all of you.

I've learned that we have a history of good guys and bad guys, people who used imagination and talent to survive, people who knew how to laugh and people who left us with good raw material.

Your Uncle Harry S., who is a textile designer, was surprised to learn about the people in our family who sewed their way to success. I was amazed to find out that there was a relative who'd had two different-colored eyes just like me. My daughter Dianne who loves a good joke and is the top-selling real estate agent in the whole state may have inherited her ancestor Ben's ability to tell jokes and turn laughter into sales! Even Donny, who started me on this project, is like our ancestor Nathan who felt a love and respect for animals of all kinds.

I'm proud to have come from this cantankerous lot.

When I look around at all of you, I see and love those very same qualities in you. [3]

Love,

Mom, Grandma, Aunt, Great-Aunt, Cousin (your choice) Sarah

Here is a portion of the family tree that Sarah created for her family. We have underlined some of the words and phrases she used to help bring her ancestors' experiences to life. As you can see, including this kind of information can add deeper value and meaning to the histories you pass along.

Ben P. (Ella's younger brother)

Came to America a year after Ella did and became a traveling salesman in upstate New York. He <u>loved telling jokes</u> and because of that he was a good salesman. He sent for Ella and her husband, Nathan, to work with him (that was <u>the beginning of their dry goods business</u>).

Ella and Nathan's oldest daughter, Ruth, married Samuel K. Ella and Nathan had six children. One of them died at birth. The others were two girls and three boys. Ruth was the oldest and <u>had one blue eye and one brown eye. She and her husband started a haberdashery</u> (hat-making store) because when Ella died she'd left a good amount of cloth and sewing tools that they could use.

❧ The Friday Journal

The man who told us the next story described another way to make sure that the people you love won't be left with their important questions unanswered. He reminded us that the words we speak don't always live on after we are gone. Sadly, it took the sudden death of his wife of twenty-seven years for him to fully understand that. Here is what he said:

Off and on over the years, my wife used to point to one little thing or another that decorated our home. Then she'd say something like, "If I die, I want you to give this to so-and-so and I want you to tell him that I picked this especially for him because ..."

Whenever she talked like that, I stopped listening. She wasn't going to die. I thought the whole thing was silly. Now I wish I had paid attention. Some nights, I walk through the house and look at her things. Once, I carried a clipboard and pencil around with me hoping I'd remember what she had said—what she had wanted me to give to her close friends and family—and why she had chosen that one thing just for them. But I couldn't remember. I couldn't pull her words back up. I won't let important moments slip by me again.

And he hasn't. As a matter of fact, this man showed us that it is possible to take what so many of us already write in our personal journals and make it even more meaningful and helpful to others.

Here is a letter he wrote to his children:

December 1998
Dear J. and M.,
For months after your mom died, the two of you were the only reason I got out of bed each day. [4] During all that time, I kept thinking of questions I wanted to ask your mom, like what she would want me to tell you when you face a challenge or reach a special milestone. I'll never know what she'd have said to you at such times, and that makes me sad for all of us.

But I'm finished sitting around and wishing for the impossible. [1] I've decided to write in this journal so that you won't ever have to wonder about what I might have said to you. [5] Every Friday after work, I am going to write down one thing that I'd like you to know about the way I see the world and each of you. I will leave it open on my bed stand, and you can read it whenever you want to.

Here it is:
Together the three of us have learned that nothing and no one lasts forever. We've learned another truth: It's important to put your love and advice in words some-where so that other people can feel your presence forever.

J., you've just started a new job and I know there will be people who will tell you that cutting corners can lead you to success faster than not. I think that cutting corners is a direct route to shoddy work and it catches up with you sooner or later. You probably already know this because you are an especially observant person [3], but I remember when I needed someone to tell me this, so I am passing it on to you now because it helped me to hear it.

M., last week I watched you perform in a new musi-cal. I saw a gleam in your eyes and knew that you love your work. Whether you continue as an actress or go in another direction, I hope you will keep putting yourself in positions that feel as satisfying as what you are doing now. When your eyes gleam, you will know that you are on the right path. So when in doubt, look in the mirror and you'll

find the answers you need. You will also see the face of the
talented and determined young woman I am so proud
of. [3]

I love you both [2],
Dad

16

Too Good to Miss

$\mathscr{A}$mong the hundreds and hundreds of messages that we looked at as we wrote this book, there were some that did not fully apply all the basic elements and yet resonated so deeply in us that we wanted to share them with you here. Perhaps this handful of messages proves the old adage that for every rule (or collection of basic elements) there is an exception.

However, what does seem to hold true—without exception—and what sets these messages apart from others that did not use all the elements is that

- the people who made them wrote in their own true voices
- they are filled with explicit goodwill
- they are either warm and funny, or so original that they connected powerfully with the receivers' hearts

We hope that as you read these you will be motivated to look for other new and interesting ways to create lasting messages.

❧ *Hello Future Grandparents*

This is a short note written by a woman who'd had a difficult pregnancy. By putting words into the mouth of her soon-to-be-born child, this woman created a funny message that turned into a touching family keepsake:

> Monday, November 5, 1979
> Dear Grandma and Grandpa,
> My parents told me that I didn't have to write you any kind
> of thank-you note, especially since I'm still in my
> mommy's stomach. They said if I did write that you'd
> probably shake your heads and say you only did what

family is supposed to do and that a thank-you note is unnecessary.

But I thought it over and decided to write anyway because I am going to be raised as a courteous young man and because I love you both already and wanted you to know that.

You've both done so much to help my parents get through a difficult few months while they waited to find out if I was healthy or not. And now you bought my mom a pretty new outfit that makes her smile just to wear, and I wanted you to know I appreciate it very much. When my parents smile, it makes me feel good, too! I understand that you are planning a party to celebrate my birth. Thank you for that gift, too! I can hardly wait to hug you both. See you in mid-March.

Your grandson,

X

P.S. Before I'm born, could you please see that my parents come up with a better name for me than X?

❥ *Rudy's Running*

Very often, parents transform their young children's messages into life-time treasures. That's what happened in this case. A young mother marked the date on something her child wrote, added a two-sentence description about what the message was intended to be and put it away for her children to see again when they are grown. Here is what this mother wrote:

10/4/90.
This is a speech that was written by "Gabrielle" when she was eight years old for her brother, "Rudy," who was ten. Rudy was running for school treasurer at the time and he (wisely) chose not to deliver this speech.
Here is what Gabrielle wrote for her brother:
Hi, I am Rudy.
I am runig for tresurer.
Please fot for me because
I'm going to try to take care of
all the Representevs tresures

❥ *Weird Spots on My Ankles*

A while ago, a friend of ours proudly showed us a small, hand-decorated, wire-bound book (about the size of an old-fashioned autograph book) that her grown daughter, Colette Stern, had made for her.

Colette had named the book *Do You Remember When?* She had varnished its front and back covers and dated it, and on the first page, she had written words of love and thanks to her mother. Then on each of the remaining pages, Colette preserved bits and pieces of dialogue from their shared past that captured moments special to them both. One page in particular seemed to leap out at us with great force. Here is that page:

> Do you remember when...
> "Mom, I have some weird spots on my ankles. I don't know what they are."
> "Are you sure they aren't just dirt or freckles? OK, we're going to the doctor." You insisted even though I resisted. And thank goodness you did. It's quite possible you saved my life.
> "You need to take your daughter over to the emergency room immediately." Wow, those were scary words. We couldn't believe we actually walked over there—then found out it could be lupus, leukemia or ITP. You kept your cool, though, and didn't let me see how scared or upset you were. We made it through everything together—foam toothbrushes, painful IV, World Series, that sweet nurse, a bone marrow test (during which I almost broke Dad's hand), a blown-up hand, my millions of questions, physical therapy (which ended up being a good science fair project) and lots of friends and family. And hey, I got a great essay for colleges and med school from it!
> Thanks for everything you did.

❥ *Exercise Your Will*

For most of us, writing a will provokes uneasy, somber feelings. However, one man showed us that it could also be an opportunity to capture the lighter, joy-filled moments we've shared along the way. Here is the note this man attached to his will:

> August 11, 1995
> Dear Sally, David, Michael and Jane,
> Besides the legal mumbo jumbo in this will, I'm adding some plain talk about the things I want you to have. They aren't worth much in terms of dollars and cents, but they mean a lot to me because they're about the times we shared. I hope they hold as much meaning for each of you and that you'll take comfort in knowing how deeply I care

about (and feel loved by) each of you. I know you are feeling sad now and there's not much I can do about that except try to leave you all with a smile. So, here it is.

Jane B., you were the "much older" girl next door. I had a crush on you when I was in the seventh grade and you were in the tenth. I'm leaving you the drawing you made for me of a dog because I figured that picture was your way of acknowledging my puppy love.

Michael M., your taste in music has always been crummy. I'm leaving you all the record albums I still have from our college years. I stored them so I wouldn't have to listen to them after you finally talked a good woman into marrying you. The music still stinks, but maybe they're worth something now since no one makes records anymore. Please sell them. Don't inflict them on your wife!

David D., I'm leaving you the cigars that are hidden in the bottom drawer of my desk. Try to convince Sally that they're yours and that I was just "storing them for you." Not that she'll believe you any more than she believed me! God bless her for never making that an issue between us.

Sally, my wonderful wife, you will have enough money to live wherever you want to. I'm leaving you my trust in any choice you make. Thank you for giving me more happiness than I had any right to expect. Miss me for a while and then get back to living as completely as I know you would want me to.

❧ *More Than the Father of My Friend*

Below is a condolence card that an acquaintance of ours, Jack Halpern, sent to a lifelong friend. We wanted you to see this card because we think it does a good job of incorporating the *I won't pretend* special element for messages of comfort with the phrase "I imagine his loss seems insufferable to you, and I am sorry about this":

October 1996
Just wanted to take a moment to let you know that I've been thinking about you a lot since the holidays and to offer condolences on the loss of your father. I imagine his loss seems insufferable to you and I am sorry about this. [I won't pretend]

I feel fortunate to have known him for the last thirty-five-plus years, and to have had a chance to interact with

him in a variety of circumstances. He was not just the
"father of my friend"—he made me feel that he was my
friend as well.

He always offered a smile and warm greetings and
brightened my path and that of everyone else he encoun-
tered. I hope the knowledge that he was beloved by so
many others in the community will be a source of
strength and comfort to you and your family in the days to
come.

Sincerely,
Jack

➤ *The Goodest Person*

Here is a letter that JacLynn wrote to her friend Barbara Mays's children.
Generally, people use the elements to reveal their feelings for the people who
will receive their messages. In this case, however, the words that reflect elements 2 and 3 do not describe JacLynn's feelings about the receivers; instead,
she used these elements to communicate her feelings for her friend Barbara
(the receivers' mother):

April 9, 1999
Dear Meredith and Michael,
I just finished reading several stories about random acts of
kindness and realized that I know an even better story
about your mom. You've probably heard me describe her
as the "goodest person in all the land." But I don't think
you know why I call her that. I'm telling you this in a letter
so that someday you can show it to your children and tell
them how your mom saved the life of a man she never
even met.

This happened about five or six years ago during the
time that your grandfather was gravely ill. Back then, your
mom spent most of her waking hours in a small room
outside the hospital's cardiac care unit waiting to be able to
sit beside your grandfather for fifteen minutes each hour,
which is all the hospital allowed. To pass the rest of each
hour, your mother talked with the other people who were
visiting their own sick relatives. That's how she met a
young woman from a tiny town in southern Georgia
whose husband had been waiting for many months for
the only thing that could save his life: a heart transplant.
And he was nearly out of time.

I knew nothing about any of this until your mom

called and said she needed my help immediately. She was so insistent that I raced over to your house and found your mother sitting on the kitchen floor surrounded by piles and piles of papers. She looked up at me and said, "I need the names of everyone you know in the press or media. I am going to call them and ask them to publicize the need for organ donations now!" I rattled off the names of local reporters and editors I knew. She took notes, and I left and forgot all about it.

A few weeks after that, I opened our local paper. On the front page of the Living section was a full-page story about the need for organ donations and there was a smaller article about a man near death who'd been waiting for a heart so long that it was now almost too late. There was no mention of your mother in the story.

But I knew she had to be behind this vivid news coverage. So I picked up the phone, called her and shouted, "You did it!"

"I did what?" she asked.

When I told her, she shrugged it off. However, a few weeks later she smiled when she told me the man had gotten a heart. I asked her what his name was. She didn't know. I asked if they knew what she'd done and she said, "Why, no. Of course not."

Your mother pulled off a quiet miracle, and that's just one of the many reasons I think she's "the goodest person in all the land." [3] She'll probably blush if you ask her about this, but I hope it makes you as proud to know her as I am. [2]

Love,

JacLynn

❧ A Grandson's Promise

This is an example of a heartfelt message of apology written by Rabbi Ronald M. Segal, assistant Rabbi at Temple Sinai in Atlanta, Georgia, to his elderly grandfather. Distressed about his own unfinished business with his grandfather and hoping to encourage others to repair their damaged relationships, the rabbi decided to read his letter aloud to his congregation. He prefaced his letter with these remarks:

Some months ago, Rabbi Steven Z. Leder of Los Angeles, California, author of several books, including The Extraordinary Nature of Ordinary Things, *conducted a workshop encouraging his fellow rabbis to reflect on* the impact of their own unfinished business. I was among those who attended Rabbi Leder's workshop, and his words inspired me to share my thoughts with you today.

I have learned that when we stop to notice the unfinished business we carry around with us day to day, year to year, we see that it involves our relationships with parents and grandparents, siblings, children, friends and co-workers. We have deceased relatives with whom we've had no closure, relationships suffering in silence, friendships broken due to mistrust, poor communication or lack of loyalty. And this unfinished business can leave our souls wounded, less whole, in need of healing.

How do we go about repairing relationships that are broken? We start with what seems like common sense. We call a relative or friend from whom we are estranged. We put pen to paper in the hopes of repairing a relationship that was once meaningful. We ask the people whom we have hurt for forgiveness.

It seems like a simple enough task, but for those of us entrenched in our stubborn and unbending ways, mustering the strength to apologize and ask forgiveness is one of the hardest things we can imagine.

My friends, let us swallow our pride, say, "I am sorry," and ask for the gift of forgiveness. I have begun this task myself in this letter to my grandfather.

What follows are portions of the rabbi's very personal and powerful letter:

10/98
Dear Grandpa,
I have meant to write this letter to you for a long time now. But because I have waited so long, the problem is I am afraid it may be too late.

Last year I promised myself that I would be more attentive, that I would call you once a week or at least twice a month to see how you were feeling, to let you know that I love you and that I was thinking of you. I did not come close to living up to that promise; I think I called you twice during the entire year and I visited even less, so infrequently that you barely know your grandson.

I am sorry that I have not been a presence or an active part of your life during these years. I am embarrassed and remorseful that I had to practically reintroduce myself to you each time I did call. I am sad that I failed to take the time out of my schedule to be a companion for you while you could still remember the stories you so desperately wanted to share.

I wish I knew more about your memories of our family, many of whom perished in the Holocaust.

Grandpa, I am asking for your forgiveness. I want you to know that my words are sincere—from the heart. I promise that this year will be different—for you, for me, for all of us.

Love from your grandson,
Ronnie

Months after sharing this letter with his congregants, Rabbi Segal smiled, pointed to a bulging file folder on his desk and told us it was filled with notes he'd gotten from people who had begun repairing their own broken ties with others.

❥ *To Signal Her Pain*

Living with chronic illness and pain, the woman whose message you are about to read decided to use flash cards to help her children understand that her mood swings and terse words did not mean that she was angry with them.

While we think that her flash cards are a very creative solution to a troubling communication problem, we are even more impressed with the note she wrote to her children to explain what she had in mind. Here is what she wrote:

August 23, 1999
Dear Angela and Brad,
It is late at night and I am still wide awake. It is not just the aches and pains that I always have that are keeping me up now. It is also my guilty conscience. I was thinking about how sweet you both are and how mean-spirited I have been to you lately.

I do not want to keep acting this way to you, the people I love most in the whole world. We all know the pain from my muscles makes me irritable and short-tempered an awful lot of the time. But I do not want it to run our lives or make me snap at you for no reason period.

Lately, especially by the time I get to the end of the day, I think my pain makes me say unkind things to you. I do not mean to hurt your feelings and I want you to know that.

I have an idea about using flash cards like a traffic sign to show you when my pain is making me crazy. I figure that if I look at the flash cards myself before I open my mouth, maybe I won't pop off at you. Anyway, it's worth a try.

So, here's the plan. I've made three different cards. The green card means I feel fine. The yellow card means I am hurting but that if I take a breath before I say anything, I can do just fine. And the red card means that I hurt so much at the moment that I can't be sure I won't bite off your heads if you ask me to make a decision right then and there.

I know this isn't a cure for our problems. I am going to try it, though, and see if it helps, and I want you to let me know if you think it is helping you, too. Kids, thanks for hanging in there with me.

I love you,
Mom

❧ The Learning Day

Occasionally, someone tells us about an experience that changes the way we think about ourselves. The story below came from Marshall Thurber, a business consultant and motivational speaker, who shared this anecdote with people who came to his seminar titled "Money and You." This story affected Paul so positively that fifteen years later when we were writing this book, he taped Marshall's retelling of it and turned it into a message that could be passed along.

This is Marshall's story of an experience he shared with his son, Rawson, who was seven years old at the time:

Back when Rawson was in second grade, I picked him up from school each afternoon. Rawson would climb into the car smiling and wave his latest test paper. His papers were always near perfect. But one day, Rawson greeted me silently. Surprised, I said, "What's up? Where are your papers?" Rawson slowly pulled out a paper that had several red marks on it where he'd gotten the answers wrong. When we got home, we sat down together and looked through a stack of Rawson's earlier test papers, and I asked him, "Which of these did you learn the most from?"

Rawson picked up the papers where he'd gotten one hundreds and said, "These. I learned that I can get everything right."

I nodded and said, "OK, then let's look at today's test. Show me the mistakes you made." Rawson pointed to them and I said, "Did you find out how to do these problems so you can get them right next time?"

Rawson nodded, "Yeah. You do this, then this and that's how."

I smiled and said, "So you learned from your mistakes! Then, which tests do you think you learned the most from, the ones where you knew how to do everything or the one where you made mistakes?"

Rawson's eyes widened. He pointed to the test with the mistakes. "This one," he said in surprise. "I guess I learned more on the one with mistakes."

I laughed and hugged him and said, "Rawson, we're spending a fortune to send you to a private school, so I want you to make as many mistakes as you can while you're there. OK?"

About a week later, I picked Rawson up from school and he climbed into the car grinning. Rawson held up a test paper with several red marks on it and said, "Boy, Dad, did I have a learning day today!"

Here are the words that Paul added to the end of this tape:

Before I heard this story about a father who saw his son's mistakes as positive and necessary parts of learning, I considered the mistakes I'd made over the course of my life as unacceptable imperfections. Whatever I set out to do, my unconscious belief was that I should be able to get it done right the first time.

Marshall's words seemed to shift things inside me. I began to look on my early failures with a sense of compassion and even pride in the things I had learned along the way.

That's the value of stories like these. They have a way of getting through to us with more impact than even the most direct conversations in which someone tells us that we're being too hard on ourselves or that there's another way to look at things.

I hope this story has helped you as much as it did me. If it has, please pass this tape on to someone else—someone you think might appreciate hearing mistakes described as opportunities.

17

Creative Ideas

$\mathcal{H}$ere you will find eleven small stories that are filled with wonderful message-making suggestions ranging from words painted on a lampshade to healing ceremonies and audiotaped recollections of someone who is no longer here. We have included these stories in hopes that they will spark your creativity as much as they did ours.

❥ *Tots on Tape*

When the parents of four young children told us how they turned memories into messages, we liked their idea and wanted to pass it on to you. This particular mother and father bought and put aside a blank videotape cassette for each of their children. Then, every year on each child's birthday, they tape their youngster answering this question: "What do you want to be when you grow up?" Their children's answers are funny and heartwarming. And the videotapes that their parents are making are likely to become special treasures for years to come.

❥ *Picture This*

Snapshots with personal messages that describe your feelings about a special time spent with someone else can make great keepsakes. A psychologist friend of ours, Harold W. Haddle Jr., who also is a proud great-uncle, told us how he captures, keeps and shares special moments. Here is what he said in the note he attached to an original poem and photo he took of his three-year-old great-niece:

July 2, 1998

Dear Lauren,

Last summer, when I spent an afternoon getting to know
you, I took this picture of your smiling face. Later, I wrote
about what that day and you mean to me. I'm saving the
photo and my poetic description of our adventure together
to give to you when you are older. You may not remember
the details of this day by then, but I've learned that special
times are worth preserving. I hope you'll think so, too.

> She was only three—I was twenty times three.
> We were playing in the creek like two kids.
> Selective she was—a girl with a discriminating taste for
> creek rocks.
> We named them, "interesting rocks."
> Feelings of joy welled up inside me as we examined her
> interesting rocks.
> What was this joy all about?
> Though years apart,
> That day our spirits were the same age.

❧ *The Light of Her Life*

We think this message is a marvelous way to preserve and pass along
things that have inspired you. Even though Brook Raflo, the young woman who
made this message, isn't an artist, she created a piece of lasting art for her mother that is likely to shine for generations to come. Here is what Brook told us:

*I had just gotten married, money was pretty tight and my mother's birth-
day was coming up. I wanted to give her something she'd love. When you
can't spend money, you just have to pull up what's in your heart and find
some way to turn that into a gift. So, Jim and I found a small table lamp
and I replaced its shade with one I made from handmade paper and dried
leaves. On the new lampshade I wrote:*

> Happy birthday to you—March 1999—Things my mother
> taught me: To say I'm sorry—To sing Marvin Gaye
> songs—To look both ways—To drive a stick shift—To blow
> huge bubbles—To tie my shoes—To like giving presents
> —To admit when I'm wrong—To love learning—To dance
> barefooted in the living room—To notice a beautiful day—
> To hug as much as possible—To be patient—To read and
> read and read—To forgive easily—To look for the best in
> people—To collect seashells—To swim—To imagine—To

be proud of my accomplishments—To love bravely—To
scramble eggs—To share—To eat broccoli—To enjoy every
age—To treat myself—To be thoughtful—To compro-
mise—To watch old movies —To try new things—To
camp outdoors—To bend the rules on special occasions—
To crave Southern cooking—To be tactful—To wear comfortable clothes—To entertain myself—To act silly in
public—To fold fitted sheets—To write sappy letters—To
listen to other people's stories—To swoon over Robert
Redford—To climb Aunt Virginia's magnolia tree—To be a
mush-head—To care for sick loved ones—To smile as
much as possible—To love women

*I know my mother loved her birthday present because she sent me this
thank-you note, which I am going to keep forever:*

March 1999
Dear Brook,
I hope someday you will be blessed to have a child like you
are to me. You have, throughout your life, found so many
ways to tell me you love and appreciate me, surprising
ways and celebratory ways, as well as quiet, gentle glances
and soft kisses that needed no translations.

   Well you've outdone yourself this time! I have cried
with joy three times already, and I've only had the lamp
for two days. There is something very sustaining about
giving someone words in print. It reminds. It remains. Although the words are about me, they really say more about
who you are and what you value. You chose to honor those
things by making them art. And you honor me by being
who you are. Thank you for all the resources (time,
money, energy, etc.) it took for you to make the lamp, and
especially for the sitting-still time, where you thought
about you and me and found the words. My spirit soars
because of you.
   Love,
   "Mommy"

❧ *So Many Musical Memories*
   When a man we know—we'll call him "Warren"—learned that his beloved
uncle had been diagnosed with an early case of Alzheimer's disease, Warren
created a remarkable tangible message that, years later, continues to be a
source of comfort to his uncle.

As simple as the idea behind this message seems to be, we found it so touching that we've included it here for you to see.

For as far back as he could remember, Warren and his uncle had shared a common love of music. Over the years, they'd gone to a variety of musical performances together. At holiday time, the gifts they often gave each other included recordings of show tunes, classical music and big band sounds.

Here is what Warren told us:

I wanted to give my Uncle Louis something that would reverberate all the way into his soul whether he remembered anything or not. So I put together an audiotape for him. On one side of the tape, I put a lot of music I knew he liked. On the other side of the tape, I recorded songs that my aunt and cousins helped me pick out. Before the start of each song, I recorded a few sentences telling him who I was, how much I loved him, what the music he was about to hear was called and why I had included this song on his tape of musical memories.

The kinds of things I put on his tape were

> ❥ *a marching band's rendition of his old college fight song*
> ❥ *the old World War II marching tune he and his army buddies sang*
> ❥ *the music he and my aunt danced to every year on their anniversary*
> ❥ *a song he used to sing when he put his kids to bed at night*
> ❥ *the theme song from his all-time favorite movie*

Anyway, you get the idea. I made that tape four and a half years ago out of sheer desperation, I guess. I'm sad to say that my uncle no longer remembers who I am. But, the last time I visited him, his nurse said that Uncle Louis listens to that tape every single day. She also said he smiles each time he hears it. I guess it isn't much, but it means a lot to me to know that even now my uncle can enjoy something I was able to give him.

❥ *A Family's Thanksgiving Promise*

After a day spent helping to set up a shelter for battered women, a family of five was so affected by the issue of domestic violence in their community that they created a message to keep and use in the future. Together they wrote and printed copies of the following prayer, which they hand out every year to the people who share Thanksgiving dinner with them.

On one side of a standard 8-1/2″ x 11″ piece of paper, they wrote about what led them to create this prayer. On the other side is the prayer itself. We've included it here because it is an original and touching way to turn an important life lesson into a tangible message that can be passed along.

Here is a copy of what the members of this family share with others each Thanksgiving:

SIDE ONE: This is a prayer that our family wrote in September of 1997 after we helped set up a shelter for women and children who had to leave their homes and flee from a violent family member. We are giving you a copy because the message is important. We hope that after we recite this prayer you will make this prayer a part of your Thanksgiving holiday from now on so that more and more of us will start to do things that make this world a better and safer place for people who need our help.

SIDE TWO: Each year at this holiday, we pause to think about all that we have and how thankful we are to be so blessed. And we smile at each other, grateful that our homes are harbors of safety.

This Thanksgiving our hearts turn to those among us who live and suffer in homes where peace has been shattered. In the past, we have been reluctant to confront this violence, afraid to interfere.

Today, however, we will admit that in this land there are women who cower in fear of their husbands; children who are sexually, physically and/or verbally abused; and senior citizens who are ignored or imprisoned in their own homes.

So, this day, as we celebrate with thankfulness, we take time out to acknowledge that some of us remain enslaved by the violence and terror of domestic abuse. Some of us at this table may be survivors. Others of us know victims or survivors of domestic violence. This year we promise to hear the unspoken fear in their silence, notice their sadness, feel their loneliness, sense their shame, understand their bitterness and reach out to share the peace we enjoy and the comforts we too often take for granted.

❧ *The Stone Sisters*

While we were writing this book, many people told us that they wanted to create messages for loved ones who'd been diagnosed with breast cancer. Working with some of these people reaffirmed our belief that the basic elements and the special *I won't pretend* element offer a helpful way to organize and express comfort. We also noticed that when people applied the elements in imaginative ways, their messages took on added impact, value and meaning.

A case in point is a message that we heard about from a woman named "Lila." Although this is a story about comfort for a woman battling breast cancer, you can use the same approach to comfort people who are suffering from any serious illness. Here are Lila's words:

> *I had just finished reading a book about rituals that renew the spirit called* Kitchen Table Wisdom: Stories That Heal *by Rachel Naomi Remen, and I kept thinking about a friend of mine named "Carmen" who was undergoing a long series of inpatient medical treatments to combat breast cancer. I wondered if her other friends might want to put a healing ceremony together for Carmen. I called a few of them and they liked the notion, so we made plans to hold a ceremony in Carmen's hospital room a few days later.*
>
> *On the night of the ceremony, as I was walking from the parking lot into the hospital, I spotted a small, smooth, round stone. Without thinking much about it, I picked it up and brought it with me to Carmen's room. The other seven women were already there.*
>
> *One of the women lit a peach-colored candle, then we turned off the overhead lights. We formed a semicircle around Carmen, who was propped up in her hospital bed. After a few uneasy moments, I remembered that stone in my pocket. I pulled it out and we passed it around from one to the other until each of us had touched it.*
>
> *Then, quietly we took turns describing a personal difficulty we had faced in our lives. Our stories were deeply personal. As much time as we had spent with one another, the things we shared that night were things we'd never told each other before. One woman spoke of having survived a brutal rape. Another woman revealed a past suicide attempt. We bared our souls and struggled to put words to the traits or beliefs that had helped us overcome and survive adversity. After that we held hands, closed our eyes and tried to will each character trait and belief that had helped us right into the stone.*
>
> *At the end of the ceremony, Carmen cradled the stone in her hands and told all of us that she felt safer and stronger in that moment than she had felt at any other time since her cancer had been diagnosed.*

Lila told us that a week following the ceremony, one of the women sent each of her "stone sisters" a written summary of their extraordinary evening to preserve their ceremony of comfort, strength and healing. We liked this idea and hope it will inspire you to do something healing when people you love are ill.

➤ *The Love Club*

This special message was posted on an Internet home page that had been set up for people who wanted to offer comfort and support to a woman who is battling a life-threatening disease called multiple myeloma. Jim Nathan, the man who created this Web site, posted the following loving message for his friend:

Sun., April 4, 1999
Dear Tricia,
I don't know anybody who has a bigger fan club than you.
(Well maybe Celine Dion beats you by a hair.) Everyone
wants to know how you're feeling, what you're going
through, how they can help and how they can express
their love. But the number one task for you, your husband
and children must be to concentrate your energy on beating this beast. That's why I've built this site, so everyone
can keep informed about multiple myeloma, offer their
support and love and comfort and their hopes and wishes
for you without your phone ringing off the hook day and
night. I hope this can be a resource for all of us and a
source of comfort to you for many, many years to come.
　　Love,
　　Jim

Among the things we like about this message are the way that Jim ac-
knowledges the seriousness of his friend's battle with her disease (without
using platitudes) and the clear and genuine manner in which he expresses his
desire to spare his friend any distractions in her war against her cancer.

❥ A Poem Shared

This message, sent by S. Stephen Selig III to a man whose father recently had died, shows how helpful it can be to pass along the things that comforted you at similar moments in your life:

September 1996
I was thinking of you and hoping you and your family will
treasure the wonderful memories your dad left behind.
　　When my father died, someone sent me the enclosed
poem. It meant a great deal to me and I hope you will de-
rive comfort from its message during your time of
sadness. Please know I will miss your father, too.
　　Sincerely, Steve

The poem that Steve included with his note is "I Follow a Noble Father" by
Emma McKay. You can find this poem on the Web at http://www.aspiring-
community.com/files/fatherhood-i-follow-a-noble-father.html.

❥ For Her Beautiful Children

There is a special way of knowing about people that comes from stories
their friends can tell. In a eulogy he delivered a few years ago, Fran Tarkenton,

NFL hall-of-fame quarterback, brought his friend Debbie vividly alive in ways that touched and delighted the people who were there to pay their last respects.

Fran talked about how dearly Debbie loved her children and explained how often he'd seen her wave pictures of them in front of strangers in order to ask, "Don't Stuart and I make beautiful children?" Fran's stories helped us picture Debbie laughing as he let her paint his toenails in red polish. He described the way she enjoyed all kinds of surroundings with equal gusto. "Whether we were in a dingy hole-in-the-wall diner seated on cracked vinyl chairs or in a plush five-star gourmet restaurant, Debbie would always say, "Isn't this the best!" And she would mean it. Near the end of his remarks, Fran told Debbie's family that he shared and understood their enormous loss and deep sorrow (an example of the *I won't pretend* element).

After the funeral, Fran said he wished he had written his eulogy on paper so that he could have given it to his friend's husband and children. "That way," he explained, "they could recall Debbie's laughter, dancing eyes, pride in her family, spirit of fun and outrageous curiosity whenever they want."

We liked Fran's idea about giving written copies of a eulogy to surviving friends and family members. It seems to us that doing that could be a wonderful gift of lasting comfort. So, we decided to pass his idea along to you.

❧ *Preserving Their Memories*

Different cultures and most religions observe special rituals of mourning. Jewish people have a heartwarming tradition that applies to the first week of mourning called sitting Shiva. During this time, people who visit with the mourners bring food, help out with chores and participate in daily worship. Perhaps one of the most important functions of this special week involves telling one another stories about the person who has died. It is considered a mitzvah (loosely translated, this is the Hebrew word for a "good deed") to share recollections about the deceased because doing that helps those who knew the person to know them even more fully. And it can give the surviving family members a great deal of comfort to hear about the impact their loved one had on others.

A few months ago, a friend of ours tape-recorded some of the stories that people told about a man who had recently passed away. The stories ranged from hilarious episodes of the deceased's wild youth to quieter moments about previously unknown charitable acts. At the conclusion of the week of sitting Shiva, our friend gave a copy of the tape he'd made to the widow of his deceased friend.

She told us this:

The fact that someone made this tape for us is extraordinary and deeply appreciated. I was in shock so much of that first week after my husband died that I barely heard a word anyone said. Now I can hear about and re-

play recollections of my husband's life whenever I want. I take a great deal of comfort in knowing how many wonderful moments he gave all of us, and this tape lets me keep some of those moments alive.

We've included this story here to encourage you to look for other creative ways to offer lasting comfort.

❥ Senior Scenes

Some special messages are meant for larger audiences than a written note might reach. Passing along the kinds of memories that can be watched by groups of people at the same time is easier than ever with today's technology. Videotaping, for example, can be a great (and affordable) way to make and keep permanent messages. And very often, videotaped messages become more meaningful as time passes.

A fellow writer and friend, Robyn Freedman Spizman, author of dozens of books, including *When Words Matter Most: Thoughtful Words and Deeds to Express Just the Right Thing at Just the Right Time,* told us this:

Back when my Great-Aunt Francie, a family favorite, was in her late eighties (at least we think that's how old she was—she'd neither confirm nor deny our suspicions), my husband and I used our video camera to capture her on tape. Later, when she died, we showed our videotaped interview to the relatives who had gathered after the funeral. It was wonderful to be able to see my great-aunt so vividly. Her image and words on tape touched us all, especially the part where she told us exactly how she hoped to be remembered.

I think one of the best things about videotaping our loved ones is this: It allows us to document their lives in lasting ways that we can hand down to future generations.

18

Starting Now

$\mathcal{T}$hank you for reading our book. We hope you will feel moved to begin sharing your wonderful thoughts, feelings and wealth of experiences in lasting ways. We believe that turning what you've learned, what you remember and your loving hopes for others into tangible messages filled with goodwill is one of the grandest acts of giving there is.

In writing this book, we discovered that there are as many reasons to create tangible messages as there are people. And, like the other people whose stories and messages you have read here, we found that making lasting messages enriched our lives as well as the lives of the people we love. But the best part of all of this—at least for us—was hearing one reluctant writer after another describe, with surprise, how easy it was to make their messages.

Our aim throughout this book has been to show you as many simple ways as we could to turn loving thoughts into lasting messages; however, there is one more point to message making that Tom Duncanson, a man we met while writing this book, makes clear in the last line of the story that follows.

❥ Today's Tender Truths

Although some people wait to express their gentle feelings and thoughts about one another until they are facing death (their own or a loved one's), Tom Duncanson chose to do things differently. And, in the process, he may have taught his children something important about the value of making and delivering personal, touching messages while we are still here.

Here is what Tom did.

He bought a video camera and used it to make a holiday message for his four grown children. Then he programmed his videotaped message to start playing the moment his children arrived on Christmas Day. When the four of them came into the room, their father was nowhere to be seen, so they settled down and watched his videotape together.

The tape showed their father standing in the same room in which they were now seated. On the tape, Tom wished them all a merry Christmas. Then he talked about the special way he calls each of his children to mind in his prayers every night.

Near the end of this touching, quietly spoken message, Tom told his children that when they turned around they would find him taping their reactions to his video message.

That's when one of his daughters, with tears in her eyes, said, "Oh, Dad, that was wonderful. I was afraid this was a message that was going to end with you telling us all that you were dying or something."

Surprised, Tom hugged her and said, "Honey, I'm sorry that's what you thought. I guess a lot of people do wait till they're about to die before they say these things. But not me!" He grinned and added, "What's the point of waiting to do that until we're dying? Sharing loving feelings is the secret to a happy life."

❥ *It's Your Turn*

Whether the loving things you'd like others to know are meant for now or for later, consider this: When we started this project, we still had time to put the best of ourselves into messages that touch, connect, heal, love, thank and cherish others. And right now, so do you.